Dealing with
DEATH

Dealing with DEATH

A CHRISTIAN PERSPECTIVE

Peter Cotterell

Scripture Union
130 City Road, London EC1V 2NJ

First published 1994

ISBN 0 86201 881 1

Unless otherwise specified, Scripture quotations in this publication are from the Holy Bible, New International Version, Copyright © 1973, 1978, 1984 International Bible Society, published by Hodder & Stoughton.

Cover design by Tony Cantale Graphics.

British Library Cataloguing-in-Publication Data
A catalogue record for this book is available from the British Library.

Phototypeset by Intype, London.

Printed and bound in Great Britain by Cox and Wyman Ltd, Reading, Berkshire.

DEDICATION

This has been a difficult book to write.

It comes from sharing with so many people the most intimate of experiences, the experience of a dawning awareness of one's own mortality:

'I, too, must die',
the experience of dying,
the experience of being with those who are dying,
the experience of bereavement.

Some of this sharing has, for me, been uplifting and even inspiring. Some has been profoundly painful.

And so I dedicate my book to those who have allowed me the privilege of sharing. They will know who they are: Julie and Ted and Mildred and Vi and Jo-Anne, and so many others over the years.

And to all those who walk through the valley of the shadow of death, in the hope that even there the light of the love of the God of all comfort will shine through.

CONTENTS

Chapter One

DEATH AND RELIGION

*For many intellectual unbelievers life is meaningless
and hopeless. They do not know where they came from,
and why they are here or where they are going.
They stumble on in the cosmic darkness.*

Billy Graham

A personal explanation

While I was writing this book a letter arrived. It was from
a relative who was trying to construct a family tree: to
find out who was born when and where, who married
whom, how many children they had, what happened to
them, and who they married. He wanted me to check
some of the details he already had and in particular he
wanted to be sure that he had my details correctly. I soon
located my own name. There it was. 'Born: 4th May 1930.'
And then underneath that: 'died: _____.' Call it
morbid if you like, but as I looked at that one word and
the blank space beside it I thought to myself, 'One day
someone will fill in that blank.'

And they will! Because death is the great certainty. Most
of us have memories of people close to us who have died
– parents, neighbours. My father died when I was just a
baby of less than two months, so I never knew him and
have no memory of his death. However, I remember the

death of my grandfather quite clearly. He used to visit us regularly, almost every week, and I can remember remarking on the curious fact that now he no longer came to visit the home. Much more vividly I recall the death of my grandmother. We boys used to cycle the five miles or so to visit her most Sundays. This particular Sunday we didn't feel like going. And, boy-like, it didn't really seem to matter very much to us. The next week there came an urgent message to my mother. She hurried off. Late that night when we were already in bed my step-father came up the stairs, opened the door to our room and said, with no preliminaries at all, 'Gran has died'. He shut the door and we could hear his steps going down the stairs again, leaving us with this mystery of death.

We didn't understand, and we couldn't even help one another to understand. I certainly had no comfort from the pious thought that Gran had 'gone to heaven', or 'gone to be with Jesus'. Our family wasn't religious. I still remember how my twin brother and I cried. I'm not sure why we cried, but we cried ourselves to sleep. Next day there was the solemn business of sewing the little black diamonds on our sleeves to show that someone in the family had died. We went off to school aware, I think, that we were a little set apart from the rest. One of the sixth formers came up, kindly, to ask what had happened. But I remember still that I couldn't explain: 'Oh, it's nothing . . . my Gran has died, that's all'.

But I had a new and deep problem to work out, the problem of death. Grandfather had died, and had gone out of our lives. Gran had been much closer to us, and now she had gone too. Dead. I began my wrestling with the obvious conclusion that everyone died, that one day I would die. I needed to deal with that unimaginable conclusion. Somewhere inside me I worked out my first theory of death as it might be expected to apply to me. I couldn't deny *death* any more. And I couldn't understand it either.

No-one ever talked about it. Perhaps mistakenly I was not allowed to see either my grandfather or my grandmother after they died. I didn't even go to the funerals. So death was a major mystery: I simply didn't have any tangible facts, anything I had *seen* that would help me to understand it.

And I wanted to understand. I had to. Of course I simply couldn't imagine a world without me, and yet now I *knew* that people died, disappeared, stopped being. How could that *disappearing* relate to me? Of course to myself I was unique, and I wanted to preserve me. It seemed necessary to the world that I should preserve me. And to preserve me, without whom the world couldn't meaningfully exist, I devised a theory: that others would die, but I would not. Somewhere along the way time would somehow stop, and leave me comfortably living day after day without ever getting older.

Eventually I outgrew that particular theory. But probably everyone, everywhere, develops a theory, an answer, a chain of theories, a set of answers, to deal with this enigma of death. That theory or those ideas usually form part of the special package we call religion.

Trying to understand death

It is certainly striking that it has proved impossible to find a people anywhere, at any point in the world's history, that didn't have a religion. Religions offer answers to the otherwise unanswerable questions, and death is perhaps the ultimate unanswerable question. Death makes life seem pointless . . . unless there is more to life than *this*. Probably there have always been some people who have simply ignored religion, denied religious answers, denied even that there *are* any answers; people prepared to accept the notion that life doesn't make sense and mustn't be expected to make sense. And even they would usually *like* it to make sense! But the rest of us struggle with the great problems of life, and its greatest mystery, death.

In the Bible there is a book which the honest Christian finds very difficult to understand. It's Ecclesiastes, 'The Preacher.' And it appears to be saying some very odd things. A recurring theme is the apparent meaninglessness of life:

> So I hated life, because the work that is done under the sun was grievous to me. All of it is meaningless, a chasing after the wind. I hated all the things I had toiled for under the sun, because I must leave them to the one who comes after me. And who knows whether he will be a wise man or a fool? Yet he will have control over all the work into which I have poured my effort and skill. . .

> I also thought, 'As for men, God tests them so that they may see that they are like the animals. Man's fate is like that of the animals; the same fate awaits them both: as one dies so dies the other. All have the same breath; man has no advantage over the animal. Everything is meaningless. All go to the same place; all come from dust, and to dust all return. Who knows if the spirit of man rises upward and if the spirit of the animal goes down into the earth?'
>
> *Ecclesiastes 2:17–19, 3:18–21*

The book of Ecclesiastes is a dialogue, first taking the part of those who leave God out of the reckoning, and showing that life simply becomes meaningless. Then accepting the consequences: life *can't* be meaningless, so there must be God. And while that doesn't answer all the questions, at least it brings into the equation someone so great that he just might be able to make sense out of it for us:

> I have seen the burden God has laid on men. He has made everything beautiful in its time. He has also set eternity in the hearts of men; yet they cannot fathom what God has done from beginning to end. I know that there is nothing better for men than to be happy and do good while they live. That everyone may eat and drink, and find satisfaction in all his toil – this is the gift of God. I know that everything God does will endure for ever; nothing can be added to it and nothing taken from it. God does it so that men will revere him.
>
> *Ecclesiastes 3:10–14*

Now that was as far as the writer could get without revelation. It represents a religion of a sort: it has humanity on one side, with all its problems, and God on the other side with all the answers. But the two can't seem to come together. I'm down here with my questions, and he's out there with the answers.

Human answers, human religions

The great religions go one step further and try to probe the mysteries of God, with human minds. Often quite brilliant human minds, but still human minds. Not surprisingly some of the answers are soon discarded. Marxism, for example, must be one of the most short-lived religions ever: Karl Marx was born in 1818, produced his book *Das Kapital* in 1867, the first Marxist state, Russia, appeared in 1917, and in 1990, just over seventy years later, Marxism was discredited, dead.

Of course some of the answers given by religions come close to the truth. Muhammad, for example, saw the absurdity of his people worshipping hundreds of different gods, of bowing down to statues and stones and animals. He grasped the fundamental fact that there is only one God.

15

The fact is that the answers given to these great issues of life and death, bundled up in human religions, are all different from one another and even contradict one another. We need revelation if we are to have clear answers to these vital issues which are simply too great for our minds to work out unaided. And in particular we can't work out the mystery of death, because those who know the answers are gone from us. My old Gran, she knows the answers. But she has gone from us and can't tell us the answers.

What we need is someone who has died, and who can come back afterwards to tell us about it. As Jesus did. Or we need someone who has watched people dying, but from the other side of the curtain we call death, and has received them into that other world which we call eternity, *and has then come here amongst us to tell us about it.* As Jesus did.

Or we need someone who has talked to Jesus. As John did, and Matthew did.

Revelation and religion

This book will be concerned with death, and with offering a *Christian* explanation of it. I offer this explanation, and not the Buddhist, Hindu or Muslim explanation because I am a committed Christian and I believe that the Christian answers are the right answers. I believe that Christianity is different from religions: it is a *revelation*. It did not appear by someone thinking about the problem of death and eventually coming up with the answer. It appeared when God became incarnate: when Jesus came amongst us human beings, talking to us, sharing with us authoritatively the right answers to absolutely fundamental questions, right answers which otherwise we could never find. So I distinguish between Christianity and the religions, between revelation and religion. Someone once asked a

Christian missionary in India: 'Look, we have our own religions, religions that are thousands of years old. What does Christianity have to add to all that?' And the missionary replied with just one word, 'Jesus'.

John Stott, in his book *The Contemporary Christian*, quotes Professor John Mbiti of Kenya: 'The uniqueness of Christianity is in Jesus Christ.' He quotes the confrontation between the Indian Sadhu Sundar Singh and an agnostic professor, who asked him what he had found in Christianity which he had not found in his old Hinduism. He responded: 'I have Christ.' 'Yes, I know,' said the Professor, a little impatiently, 'but what particular principle or doctrine have you found that you did not have before?' 'The particular thing I have found is Christ.' Stott also quotes Bishop Stephen Neill, who was a missionary in India and Africa: 'The old saying "Christianity is Christ" is almost exactly true. The historical figure of Jesus of Nazareth is the criterion by which every Christian affirmation has to be judged.'

Jesus really *is* unique. Gautama, who founded Buddhism, Muhammad, who founded Islam, Abraham who is the father of Judaism, and Confucius . . . they did not claim to be God. *Jesus did.* When his follower Thomas *saw* Jesus alive after his crucifixion he exclaimed, 'My Lord and my God!' And Jesus didn't tell him not to use such language. On the contrary, he praised him for it, and praised all those who in the centuries to come would say the same thing, without even having the advantage of seeing him (John 20:28). Ordinary people, extraordinary people, honest and sincere people have founded religions. But they are just that: religions, human ideas. Jesus brought not another religion, but revelation, reliable information from God. After all, he is the only one who *knows*.

The search for meaning

Throughout history we have been trying to find the answers to our questions about life and death and the world beyond death. Muhammad spent the night hours in a cave outside the city of Mecca and eventually brought back the explanation he believed God had given him. Gautama the Buddha sat beneath the fig tree, 'the tree of enlightenment,' as it came to be called, and eventually came up with his explanation. Karl Marx retired to the British Museum, and eventually produced *Das Kapital*, which was his explanation of the mystery of life and death.

About death each said something different. Now I call these *religions*, and label them as human ideas and not as revelations, precisely because the answers are all thought out by individuals, people of varying background, limited knowledge, mixed motives, and because *the answers they give are not merely different, they are contradictory. They can't all be correct. If they were all of them revelations then they would all agree and they could all be correct.* But they don't all agree, they can't all be correct. So I want to share with you what I understand as not just another religion, but as a unique revelation, given to us not by yet another prophet, but by God incarnate, Jesus of Nazareth.

Death and life

In my lifetime I've been involved in four murders. In one I was on the jury trying the case. In another I had to go to the mortuary to collect the body of one of the people killed. The third was the murder of a fellow missionary in Ethiopia, and I had to conduct the funeral service. Each one of them illustrated in some sense the apparent meaninglessness of life: life suddenly, unexpectedly, inexplicably cut off by violent death.

But the fourth murder case, involving the murder of a woman and the attempted suicide of the murderer, illustrates it most unforgettably. In a quiet London suburb I was driving my daughter, Anne, to school. I turned into the road where the school was situated. And there on the grass verge were two people, a man and a woman, struggling together. They collapsed on the ground. I stopped the car, hurried Anne into the school playground, ran back across the road to find a horrific mess: blood everywhere, two people, one apparently dead, the other near to it. Other people arrived. We did what we could and eventually an ambulance arrived, then the police.

It was several days before the whole picture began to emerge. The couple had been living together for several years but had not married. They had a baby and the baby began to grow up. But on this day the woman announced that she had had enough. She was leaving him. After breakfast she took their little girl off to school. He waited a few minutes, pulled a knife out of the kitchen drawer, followed her up the road, waited until she came out of the school, came up behind her, thrust the knife into her back and then took that same knife and cut his own throat. She was dead on arrival at the hospital. He survived, and was sentenced to life imprisonment for her murder. *And inside the school was a little girl, whose world had just collapsed about her. Death had snatched away her mother. Because of that death her father was gone, too. So how do you explain that?*

There is no arguing with that last enemy, death. It is so utterly final. You can't even *question* death. But how do you explain that to a bewildered little girl? Death, which up to that moment had been an irrelevancy, suddenly had shown its ultimate power, its ultimate importance. And it didn't seem to make much sense to any of us in any way involved in that murder.

Oddly enough it is death that gives significance to life. Death warns us that life does not go on for ever. Just so many years, and no more. If life went on for ever it would simply be absurd, even boring; a meaningless, bad joke. But because life goes on for only fifty, sixty, seventy years, with death at the end of it, every one of those years of life has its own special significance. The choices that I make in life are given significance by the fact that I must die, that the time will come when I will have no more choices to make.

The years are too few to be wasted in the totally trivial. I want to accomplish something before the books are balanced and the final assessment of my performance is made. In fact, even people who think that after this life there is nothing, still often want to do something significant with the one life that they have. And probably most of us get to the end of life feeling that we haven't understood what life was all about, that we haven't made out of life all that life could have been. Life is ended, but it is unfinished:

> It is not finished, Lord, there is not one thing done;
> There is no battle of my life that I have truly won.
> And now I come to tell thee how I fought, to fail,
> My human, all too human tale
> Of weakness and futility...
>
> I cannot read this writing of the years,
> My eyes are full of tears,
> It gets all blurred, and won't make sense;
> It's full of contradictions, like the scribblings of a
> child,
> such wild,
> wild hopes and longings as intense as pain,
> Which trivial deeds make folly of – or worse.
>
> I can but hand it in, and hope
> That thy great mind, which reads the writings of so
> many lives,

Will understand this scrawl and what it strives to
say,
But leaves unsaid.
I cannot write it over, the stars are coming out,
My body needs its bed. . .
I have no strength for more,
So it must stand or fall –
Dear Lord –
That's all.

(Kennedy, 1927, p 92)
Used by permission

Those of us who believe that we have just one life, and
then comes this experience called death, and then we still
have to face God's assessment of that one life, and after
that again there is another kind of life altogether, well, we
see death as enormously significant. It's not just a question
of the record we leave behind that concerns us, but much
more the record that we carry forward through the gateway of death. It's not just a question of what people here
may think of us, but much more it's what God there
will think of us. *That's* what gives life and death their
importance.

Chapter Two

ONE THING YOU CAN BE SURE OF

Mother Teresa looks past the physical features of every needy man, woman or child, and she says that she sees the face of Jesus staring up at her through them... Surrounding every lonely dying man she cradles in her arms is Jesus.

Billy Graham

We all have to die. That's the great certainty. As we get older so the parts of our bodies begin to wear out. Some parts are readily replaceable: skin is dying all the time, and is continually being replaced. White blood corpuscles fight their wars against invading germs and die, but the marrow in our bones gets to work and produces more white blood corpuscles.

Other parts are less easily replaced. The body is a bit like a car: there are parts that can be replaced. The wise owner not only keeps the bodywork in good shape, checks regularly on the oil level, battery, tyre pressure, and cleans up the odd spot of rust as it occurs, but also replaces the parts that wear out. But eventually any car *that is used* will have major problems. The day will come when it won't pass the MOT no matter what. Time for a new car! And it's the same with the human body. It has a number of major trouble spots. The heart, obviously. And the brain, the body's command centre. The blood circulation system is highly vulnerable to trouble: a mass of thread-like tubes through which the blood is pumped, twenty-four hours a day, seven days a week, fifty-two weeks in the year, from birth until ... until the pumping stops. Stopped by a blockage, probably caused by the diet we people in the western world have been persuaded into eating. So one day the whole system is clogged up and the heart refuses to keep pumping.

So we all have to die. Well, obviously. Otherwise the world would very soon be packed tight with people. Even from the very beginning there must have been some kind of 'death' intended for us. But probably not the kind of death that we have to face up to now. Death as we know it now is an intruder, it's not what God intended for us. So where does this present kind of death come from?

Why must death be like this?

To answer the question we have to go back in history quite a long way. It seems to me that we can't really understand this world without accepting the idea of a 'fall' of some kind. Human behaviour is simply inexplicable otherwise. When the world was first created God saw that it was all 'very good' (Genesis 1:31). It all made good sense. But it doesn't make good sense any more. In fact some of the things that we do to one another are almost unbelievably wicked. In the newspapers today, as I write these words, is the story of the first man to be hanged for murder in the United States of America for some thirty years. In an almost unimaginably appalling way he tortured, abused and then murdered three children. The last of them, a four year old, he assaulted and tortured, and then deliberately left alive overnight so that he would be better able to enjoy the killing in the morning. Men and women involved in this case required long term psychiatric care to deal with the shock of the experience. Why do people do these terrible things?

The answer is to be found in the Christian idea, the Bible idea, of a 'Fall': that the world has 'fallen' from what it was meant to be. I don't very much mind *how* you decide to interpret those opening chapters of the Bible – the story of creation, and of Adam and Eve and then the story of the first murder, Abel murdered by Cain – but unless we take its message seriously we'll never be able to understand the world. We are a fallen people, and we live in a fallen world. This world is not the way it was meant to be. 'God saw all that he had made and it was *very* good', but just five chapters further on in Genesis and we have a different view:

> The Lord saw how great man's wickedness on the earth had become, and that every inclination of the thoughts of his heart was only evil all the time. The Lord was grieved that he had made man on the earth, and his heart was filled with pain.
>
> *Genesis 6:5–6*

And then at the other end of the Bible we find a new world: 'there will be no more death or mourning or crying or pain, for the old order of things has passed away' (Revelation 21:4), and *that* will be very good. But in between Genesis 1 and Revelation 21 is the world that we know, this world where there are wars and where people hate one another, and there are tears and pain, and where we all have to die. A fallen world. It is not the way it was meant to be, and it is not the way that one day it will be. Human beings are not what they were created to be. But God has stepped into the world, Jesus has died for us, and now the consequences of the Fall have been dealt with. The task of putting things right has begun. We can be different. We won't be perfect but we can be better. We can be different and we can make the world different, too;

a little more as it was intended to be. But for the present this world is a fallen world.

And death as we know it now is part of that fallen world. My guess is that death was meant to be nothing more terrifying than promotion from this perfect world into the other perfect world; a step through a doorway from this world into the next, with no illness, no pain, no tears. The Fall changed all that and death became something to be feared, the last enemy. Beyond death was darkness, not light and God seemed to be no longer a loving Creator, but a frightening judge.

Immortality

Only God is immortal, undying. We are not: we must all die. But we need to ask who this 'we' is. It is important not to make the mistake of thinking that 'we' are immortal *souls* trapped in mortal *bodies*. We are people, created by God, *bodies-and-souls*. Not even *souls-with-bodies*, as though the soul is important but the body is not, or as though the soul is *immortal* and the body is not. We are *bodies-and-souls*. The idea of the immortality of the *soul* is a Greek idea (see, for example, John Stott, wrestling with the problem of heaven and hell, in David Edwards and John Stott, *Essentials*, p 316, and especially the long and invaluable discussion of the problem of the afterlife in Donald Guthrie, *New Testament Theology*, pp 828–35). The ancient Greeks believed that the body is evil but the soul is good. Death for them meant the experience of having the *soul* set free from the evil *body*.

Many Christians have taken on this Greek idea that the body is evil. Maybe they have been misled by the reference in the King James Version translation of Philippians 3:21 to our *vile* bodies. But the more modern translations get it right: they are *lowly* (RSV) or *humble* (NEB), or *weak, mortal* (GNB) bodies. The teaching of the Bible is *not* that they will be disposed of, or destroyed, but that they will be *changed*. So biblical belief is not concerned with the idea of the immortality of the soul but with the resurrection of the body, which is to be united with the redeemed spirit so that the *whole person* is set free from mortality, from death, and brought into the eternal Kingdom of God.

In particular Paul points to our resurrection as being the moment when we are *given* immortality: 'For the perishable must clothe itself with the imperishable, and the mortal with immortality' (1 Corinthians 15:53). The word Paul uses here is *athanasian*, 'not-death', which is a fascinating parallel to a very similar Old Testament statement:

> In the way of righteousness there is life;
> along that path is immortality.
>
> *Proverbs 12:28*

and the Hebrew word translated 'immortality' is *'al-mawet'*, 'not-death'. So the way of righteousness is the path to immortality; by contrast, to live in defiance of God is the path of death.

Another word that is used in the New Testament to illustrate immortality is the word 'incorruptible', *aphthartos* and its related *aphtharsia*, 'incorruptibility'. It is the opposite of corruption, decay. Death means decay. I well remember what was probably my first encounter with death. It was during World War II. We were released from school to help the farmers get in their harvest and were staying in a beautiful mansion near the Warwickshire village of Snitterfield. I was walking in the field near to the house when I saw, lying on the ground, a dead bird. Very dead. That dead bird taught me the shortness and futility of life, and it taught me the meaning of corruption. It was a putrid mass of corruption. But I am made of the same stuff! I share in that bird's mortality! But against all that there is the power of God,

... who has saved us and called us to a holy life –
not because of anything we have done but because of
his own purpose and grace. This grace was given us
in Christ Jesus before the beginning of time, but it
has now been revealed through the appearing of our
Saviour Christ Jesus, who has destroyed death, and
has brought life and immortality to light through the
gospel.

2 Timothy 1:9–10

Today death comes to us from a car smash, from illness,
from bomb or bullet ... or simply from some part of this
frail old body wearing out.

We all have to die, Christianity offers something new, a
fresh start for me, a new creation. Immortality!

Universal hope

Throughout history almost everybody has believed that
there is life after death. Even thousands of years ago relatives of the dead regularly provided them with what they
were thought to need in the new life:

> The corpses were not only carefully laid in specially
> prepared graves, but they were equipped with tools,
> ornaments and food. The significance of the custom
> is plain: the dead were thought still to be in need of
> such things ... it shows that at the very dawn
> of human culture death was not accepted as the
> definitive end of the life of the individual.
>
> *(Brandon, pp 1–2)*

Cooking pots, paper money and clothes were provided.
And there have often been special meals, eaten by the
relatives, at the graveside; meals that were in some sense
eaten 'with' the dead person. Egypt's Pharaohs got the top

treatment: huge pyramids as tombs, honeycombed with rooms, filled with furniture, jewellery, clothing and food. In Mesopotamia it seems that sometimes even the servants of the dead man were buried with him, to provide him with servants in the next life.

Universal fear

It is also true that throughout history *people have been afraid of death*. Just a few have been bold enough merely to be curious, like the Greek philosopher Socrates. He was condemned to death for allegedly perverting the morals of his students because he disbelieved in the traditional Greek legends about the gods. Socrates appears to have taken his death sentence remarkably calmly. Before the time arrived to drink the poison his friends asked him how he wished to be buried:

> 'Any way you like . . . that is, if you can catch me and I don't slip through your fingers. . . I can't persuade Crito that I am this Socrates here who is talking to you now . . . he thinks that I am the one whom he will see presently lying dead; and he asks how he is to bury me! As for my long and elaborate explanation that when I have drunk the poison I shall remain with you no longer, but depart to a state of heavenly happiness, this attempt to console both you and myself seems to be wasted on him. . .' [And when the cup of poison was brought to him] he received it quite cheerfully . . . without a tremor, without any change of colour or expression . . . quite calmly and with no sign of distaste, he drained the cup in one breath.

In fact, if the traditional account of his death is anything like correct he seems to have spent his final moments comforting and encouraging everyone else. But Socrates is rather an exception. Most people are afraid to die, afraid of death, and afraid of the dead.

Dietrich Bonhoeffer was a Christian who knew how to die. Implicated in the plot to assassinate Hitler and so bring an end to the war, the plot failed and he was arrested. In the closing weeks of the war he was condemned to be hanged:

> The last picture that we have of Bonhoeffer comes from the prison doctor, who wrote many years later:
>
> On the morning of the day, some time between five and six o'clock, the prisoners . . . were led out of their cells and the verdicts read to them. Through the half-open door of a room in one of the huts I saw Pastor Bonhoeffer, still in his prison clothes, kneeling in fervent prayer to the Lord his God. The devotion and evident conviction of being heard that I saw in the prayer of this intensely captivating man moved me to the depths.
>
> So the morning came. Now the prisoners were ordered to strip. They were led down a little flight of steps under the trees to the secluded place of execution. There was a pause. For the men about to die, time hung a moment suspended. Naked under the scaffold in the sweet spring woods, Bonhoeffer knelt for the last time to pray. Five minutes later, his life was ended.
>
> (*Bosanquet, pp 277–8*)

Death's three unknowns

Our fear of death is usually explained in terms of three unknowns: we do not know *when* we will die, we do not know *how* we will die, and we do not know what happens *after* we die (Hampe, 1979, p 5). And these concerns and fears grow as we ourselves get older. Friends die, and funerals take place with alarming frequency. There's the chilling feeling, 'Well, mine can't be far off!' Death-the-inevitable becomes death-at-hand. If only we knew *when*! Then we would know how much time we have, and we might be reassured with the knowledge that *my death* is not imminent. And if only we knew *how*! If only we could know that death would come quickly, painlessly, without announcing its coming. But then if I knew when and how, it would be even more terrifying since the when must eventually become soon, and the how, however swift, must be anticipated and savoured, and resisted. And then what if the *after* involves some kind of judgment? How could anyone face up to that prospect, at least the prospect of a *real* judgment by someone who really knew all the facts about me and my life? The possibility of *knowing* turns out to be no less fearsome than the experience of *not knowing*.

But what about the Christian and death? For nineteen years I was a missionary in Ethiopia, and I shall always remember my first Ethiopian funeral. I was up in the north of the country, in a village, learning the language. One day I went out, practising the little bit of Amharic that I had managed to pick up. Along the path came a funeral procession. Now I could *see* what the Bible had *hinted at*, the noise, the screams, the cries of pain and anguish, the picture of the dead man waved around in a frenzy of fear, the mourners tearing at their bodies, literally beating their breasts (see Mark 6:38). And the whole picture showing the hopelessness of death.

But then a few weeks later I encountered my first Ethiopian *Christian* funeral. Again a tiny village, this time in the south of the country. An elderly lady had died. We stood by the side of the path near to where the grave had been dug. We heard the sound of singing, and then the little procession appeared, dignified, singing one of the

Christian songs in the local antiphonal style. The leader makes up the chorus for everyone else to sing, and then he sings the verse, which he makes up as he goes along. It was a song about death and heaven and Jesus. At the grave there was a 'sermon' – I suppose that's what you would call it. An explanation of the difference that Christianity made to these people when it came to the time to die. An explanation of how it was that for them the fear was gone.

That was one of the great lessons I learned in Africa, and one of the lessons we seem to have failed to learn in the western world. We are still afraid of death. Genuinely, honestly, it seemed to me that the Ethiopian Christians were not afraid to die. They shared Paul's 'odd' idea that 'to live is Christ, and to die is gain' (Philippians 1:21, RSV). Paul really meant that and, as if that wasn't enough, he added that he really didn't know which was better, life or death: 'I am hard pressed between the two. My desire is to depart and be with Christ, for that is far better'!

We shall not all die

But there are some people who will not die. This world won't just fizzle out, and won't just be blown up. One day it will be wound up by God, who will send Jesus back here once more to announce the end of time, to take away his church, and to start the long process of judgment.

This is a major theme of the New Testament. Jesus himself told his followers about it and much of what he said has been kept for us (Luke 21:5–36). He didn't picture the world getting gradually better. He didn't suggest that gradually, as we became better educated and better governed wars would disappear. In fact he indicated that things would not really change much: if anything they might even get worse. And he never suggested that being a Christian would be easy. He knew only too well that when light shines the darkness tries to put it out. When honesty appears, the shoddiness of deception becomes apparent, and the shoddy-minded don't like it. When love comes, hate's bitterness can no longer be concealed, and hate is strong enough to destroy what it hates. Sadly no-one can make us *love*. We can be made to obey, but not to love. And according to the Bible love and hate will live side by side, darkness and light will struggle together, and darkness will never put out the light. But in the end a greater light will shine:

For the Lord himself will come down from heaven, with a loud command, with the voice of the archangel and with the trumpet call of God, and the dead in Christ will rise first. After that, we who are still alive and are left will be caught up together with them in the clouds to meet the Lord in the air. And so we will be with the Lord for ever. Therefore encourage each other with these words.

1 Thessalonians 4:16–18

Chapter Three

OLD AGE

An unbeliever only sees a hopeless end to life...
Malcolm Muggeridge reflected that a true Christian is
'longing for the termination of life in time as one longs
for the end of a long and arduous voyage when one
is in the last three days. I look forward to the time
when my life will partake of eternity with near
irrepressible eagerness ...'

Billy Graham

Ted Gray's sermon

Just recently I was on holiday in the southern Cotswolds, in amongst the little villages over to the south east of Cirencester. On Sunday my wife and I went to the parish church of the village of Poole Keynes for Evensong. The congregation stood respectfully as the clergy came in to begin the service. One was the Rector, a youngish man; the other an old man, almost bald (he joked about it during the sermon), but with a neat white beard: the Reverend Edward ('Ted') Gray. He was eighty-five years old, and this was to be his last sermon to the congregation he had preached to for many many years. He was moving into sheltered accommodation.

I hadn't quite bargained for this. An old man's farewell! To make things worse I had already noted that the hymn board indicated the same hymns that we had sung at Matins in the neighbouring parish of Somerford Keynes. As I suspected the readings, too, were the same. Gamely we ploughed through the repeat performance: the same prayers, the same responses, the general confession, the Lord's Prayer (twice: four times in a day was a bit beyond a joke) and then the sermon.

Ted's eyes were bad, so the Rector stood by to read the verses Ted had chosen to comment on in this his final sermon. Ecclesiastes chapter twelve:

Remember also your Creator in the days of your
youth
before the evil days come,
and the years draw nigh, when you will say,
'I have no pleasure in them';
before the sun and the light and the moon and the
stars are darkened
and the clouds return after the rain;
in the day when the keepers of the house tremble,
and the strong men are bent,
and the grinders cease because they are few, and
those that look
through the windows are dimmed,
and the doors on the street are shut;
when the sound of the grinding is low,
and one rises up at the voice of a bird,
and all the daughters of song are brought low;
they are afraid also of what is high,
and terrors are in the way;
the almond tree blossoms,
the grasshopper drags itself along
and desire fails;
because man goes to his eternal home,
and the mourners go about the streets;
before the silver cord is snapped,

or the golden bowl is broken,
or the pitcher is broken at the fountain,
or the wheel broken at the cistern,
and the dust returns to the earth as it was,
and the spirit returns to God who gave it.

Ecclesiastes 12:1–7, RSV

It was with great dignity that Ted spoke: of what old age meant to him, and of what death meant to him now that he was, by common consent, an old man, retiring from a lifetime of work for God. Ecclesiastes was right. Old age was everything that was described there. There never seemed to be enough light now to see by: every day was cloudy and overcast. The once-strong hands, 'keepers of the house', trembled now and the firm, straight legs were bent. False teeth for twentieth-century man at least kept the grinders going and made an interesting diet possible. Hearing aids made it possible to hear and, by a simple turn of a switch, as conveniently possible not to hear!

I began to see the picture of old age that the author of Ecclesiastes, that other Preacher, was trying to create. He was obviously an old man himself: he knew what he was talking about. Old age is in some ways a joke in the worst possible taste. One is young and ignorant, and at the same time one is full of self-confidence. One is a little older, and aware of just how little one knows. One learns – out of books, but even more out of experience: accidents, ill-nesses, sorrows, pains, regrets, joys, laughter, happiness. And so one begins to attain maturity. But then, old age. Fading eyesight, shaking legs, uncertain memory. The pathetic picture of the great King David in his old age, provided with a female hot water-bottle to keep him from dying of cold (1 Kings chapter 1)!

Nowadays we can order up the hip replacements, the spectacles, the hearing aids, the pep pills and the tranquil-lisers, the diets and the skin tonics, but the threat of the three score years and ten doesn't go away even if it is pushed back to three score years and twenty.

All that Ted admitted. And what did he think about death?

'It's going to be a great experience.'

I'd not really thought of it like that. A great experience. Well, of course it will be. And we need to prepare ourselves for that great experience.

'My bags are packed'

That was the comment of Pope John Paul II about old age and dying: 'My bags are packed'. It's an interesting comment. Not a despairing comment, because he was aware that death is not an end, nor even a beginning, but it is a change. And he knew that we don't move forward with *nothing*. The old saying that there are no pockets in a shroud may be true, but still some things go with me. My relationships with people: good relationships and bad ones. Maybe I'm not ready yet to have those relationships ended, just as they are, and to have them carried into eternity. Perhaps there's something to be dealt with there. My relationship with God: deep and trusting, shallow and fearful, non-existent and careless, defiant?

We all know that death has to come to us some day and yet so few of us are in the least prepared for it. So many of us are simply not ready for what must come to us eventually. And yet we could be ready. We *should* be ready.

John Wesley was once asked what he would do if he discovered that he was to die at twelve o'clock the following night. How would he spend the intervening time?

'Why, just as I intend to spend it now. I should preach this evening at Gloucester, and again at five tomorrow morning; after that I should ride to Tewkesbury, preach in the afternoon and meet the societies in the evening. I should then repair to friend Martin's house, who expects to entertain me, converse and pray with the family as usual, retire to my room at ten o'clock, commend myself to my heavenly Father, lie down to rest, and wake up in glory.'

Clearly John Wesley had his bags packed.

A friend of mine had a stroke, and was taken into hospital. He was very ill, barely conscious. I was with him when his wife, Mildred, said to him, softly:

'You know you are very ill. Is there anything you want me to do? Anyone you want me to write to? A message to someone?'

Graham lay quietly. Thought for a moment, then gently shook his head, 'No, nothing.'

Graham had lived so at peace with others, keeping such short accounts, that at the end of it all there were no last-minute adjustments to be made. He lapsed into unconsciousness, and woke up in glory.

I doubt whether too many of us are as prepared as Graham was. So it may be a good idea to start our preparations for the journey by dealing with some of the unfinished business we are leaving behind. I try to ensure that I clear up my debts as I go, so that my wife Geraldine won't have any unexpected bills to face when I've gone. But there are other debts, too: the disagreements that could so easily be settled if only we could be persuaded to start on them.

I remember one such disagreement. I was a missionary on leave from Africa. The church of which I was a member had no caretaker. One of the deacons was responsible for ensuring that the cleaning work was done, somehow. Now the Minister and I noticed that the floor of the church hall was looking a bit tatty. So we decided to polish it. We set aside a day for this major operation. We washed the floor down, we stripped off the old polish, we put down some new polish. We buffed it and polished it until that floor just shone. No, really, it looked great. It *was* great. But to our astonishment the deacon was really annoyed. Why hadn't we asked him first? It was his responsibility, not ours. A deacon criticising the Minister and the Missionary! And we, *we*, and no others, we had been gracious enough to polish floors! I fear that I, at any rate, was fearfully conscious of my humility in doing all that cleaning work, and proud of it. The weeks passed, but fellowship between us was spoiled. And one day I decided that I had had enough. I realised that I was at fault. He was quite right. Our action implied criticism of him. We should have checked with him first. For all we knew he might have had, probably did have, a schedule for dealing with the floors. I got on my bike, rode down to where he lived, rang the doorbell. He answered the door, and at once he knew why I had come: 'I'm sorry!' So easy. So soon settled. And settling some of those things may be necessary as part of our packing.

We may well need help to pack our bags. No, that's not morbid, just sensible. We have to die at some time. We don't know when. So let's be prepared: by feeling free to confront the fact of death, to be able to talk about it; to be aware of the facts about dying and death, but also to know something about what we expect afterwards. We won't be lying in a grave somewhere, waiting for resurrection, nor in some kind of limbo, neither alive nor dead, waiting for who knows what. But *we will be marvellously alive, all the restrictions of the present life gone*. Again to quote Paul:

No eye has seen, no ear has heard,
no mind has conceived
what God has prepared for those who love him.

1 Corinthians 2:9

He is talking about our salvation: and reminding us that our understanding of what it means to be saved is hopelessly inadequate. We don't realise what God *is doing* for us now, still less can we have any idea of what he *will do* for us when eventually we reach home.

And we do need to *start* packing our bags. There are arrangements to be made and there are letters to be written. For example it's simply good stewardship, and saves others a great deal of trouble, to make a will. Probably it's best to have this drawn up by a solicitor. If you decide to do it yourself, don't use a lot of technical language, keep it simple, and in any case get some advice. I prepared my will several years ago. More recently I've also written out my preferences so far as a funeral is concerned. It was when Geraldine's mother died that I discovered how much of the funeral arrangements can be in our own hands – we don't have to hand over everything to the undertaker.

But there's more to this business of writing letters than wills and funerals. There are the people we are leaving behind to think about. It must be twenty years ago now that Colin, who was a fellow student with me at Spurgeon's College, died. Like me he was a missionary, and went to Sri Lanka while I went to Africa. He was about my age. He was travelling back to London from a conference where he had been one of the speakers and on the motorway his car broke down, so he pulled over on to the hard shoulder and got out to see what the problem was. A lorry on the inside lane of the motorway smashed into him and killed him. The driver probably never knew that he had done it. Colin was about forty years old then. I was deeply touched to learn later, that even at that age he had prepared a letter to be given to his wife if something like that should happen. His bags were packed.

We can pack our bags in another way. By expanding our souls. Before I go on a journey I almost always have some kind of contact with the places I expect to visit. I write letters, receive letters, make phone calls, talk to people who know the place, get advice. And I think that there is a spiritual parallel. If I believe that I am going to God then it makes sense to get to know him better. If I know that I have seventy or so years down here but eternity with God, then it would seem to make sense to devote a bit of the seventy years to finding out about the eternity bit. I suppose that the lady who, at the age of eighty, announced that she was taking up the study of Hebrew so that she would be able to address her Creator in his own language, was a bit over the top. But the idea was right. Do I speak his 'language'? Have I started work on this whole marvellous business of being what the Bible calls 'holy' or have I put that off to Sundays and eternity? If so, then it isn't very surprising if heaven seems rather remote and even improbable. One great way to expand our souls is to cultivate prayer! I won't advise you to 'find time for it', because you never will *find* time for God. You have to carve time out of each day and allocate it to God. And when you give him that extra time God will be able to tell you a little more about how to pack your bags in preparation for eternity.

We can also help one another to pack our bags as we share with one another what God has so far done for us. I've often said to students: 'In one sense it gets easier to be a Christian as you get older, because *you know that it works*'. Younger Christians can have faith to believe that Christianity works, but they can't possibly *know* for certain that it works. It hasn't yet been tested and proved in their lives. And that's one reason why it is good for younger Christians and older Christians to get together, and for the older ones to tell their tales, to bring out their memories of what God has done. It will strengthen their own faith and it will certainly strengthen the faith of those who listen. So we can all be helped to get our bags packed.

Death is a certainty and old age is a reminder of it. But as Derek Kidner commented:

> Death has not yet reached out to us;
> let it rattle its chains at us
> and stir us into action.

(Kidner 1976, p 104)

Chapter Four

THROUGH THE DOOR

*... war does not increase the amount of death in the
world because with or without war death is universal
in every generation. Everybody dies.*

Billy Graham

Be sure of this

A few years ago I had one of the most interesting, most
absorbing, experiences of my whole life. I was summoned
to appear at the Central Criminal Court, London's famous
Old Bailey, to serve on the jury. All the officials there did
their best to make the seriousness of the occasion obvious
to us. Clerks warned us not to be late: that would be
contempt of court. Ushers warned us not to get lost in the
labyrinth of floors and corridors: that would be no excuse
if we then held up the court's activities. Solicitors bustled
around looking important. Barristers walked around looking busy. And eventually I was directed to Court Number
Two and a murder trial.

For two weeks we sat there all day listening to the
evidence, listening to the prosecution witnesses, and then
hearing them cross-examined. Then listening to witnesses
for the defence, and having *them* cross-examined. And
then the trial was over and the time had come for the jury
to come to a decision: guilty, or not guilty. Before he sent

us away to consider our verdict the judge, the Recorder of London, instructed us about our task. We must be sure. How sure?

> 'Well, let me remind you that there is only one thing in life of which you can be completely sure. . .'

He had my attention anyway, but this intrigued me: only one thing of which we could be certain? He paused, no doubt for dramatic effect. Then:

> '. . . and that is, that you must all die.'

That is the great certainty, and it is vital that if there is any sure knowledge about death and what happens after it, then we need to have it.

This chapter is mainly biblical. It has to be, because I've never been through the doorway we call death, and neither have you. To know what it's all about we depend on two things: whatever God has chosen to reveal to us, and whatever the one who has been through death and come back to talk about it cares to tell us.

We'll start with the revelation bit, and then look at what Jesus does to add to that and to confirm it.

When it comes to talking about death there are two really important parts of the Bible, both written by Paul, and both written to the same church, the church at Corinth. The first is rather well known because it's usually read at Christian funeral services. The second is less well known.

1 Corinthians chapter 15

In the first letter he wrote to the church at Corinth, Paul works his way through a long series of problems that the church had, until eventually he reaches this question of death. Chapter fifteen is a kind of climax to the whole letter. He has dealt with all kinds of problems: leadership in the church, immorality amongst Christians, getting married, where to buy meat, speaking in tongues, love, prophecy, women in church. All those issues that we study and discuss and try to explain. Some of them important, and some actually not very important at all. The fact is that we only really see what's important and what isn't when we set it in the context of death. If I'm going to die tomorrow then the colour of the carpet in the hallway or the make of car that my neighbour has just bought, or where my wife bought the joint aren't that important. But the fact that I've just had a row with my husband over the colour of the carpet, or have been criticising my neighbour's taste in cars matters a great deal. So all the problems of the Christians at Corinth must eventually be looked at in the light of the fact that they all had to die. Then they would know just how much importance each issue really had.

The fact is crucial. But what happens afterwards? There's the rub! If there's nothing at all afterwards, no further life to be lived and no God to be faced then I am free to get the most out of this life and everybody else had better get out of my way. But what if there is something else? What if there is a God to be faced, a judgment to reckon with? What if I'm going to be asked to explain why I trampled over everyone else in order to get my own way? Well then I'd best find out how God who is going to judge me expects me to live, and then live that way.

But who can tell me the truth? What are the odds on there being a God? The philosopher Blaise Pascal saw it in terms of a man sitting on a high wall. On one side is belief in God and life lived in the light of that belief. On the other side is unbelief, and life lived in a very different way. But you can't stay on the wall. You must come down, eventually, on one side or the other. Pascal actually decided that the chances were about even: taking all things into consideration it's about as likely that there is a God as that there isn't a God. But now, said Pascal, consider the consequences of getting it wrong. If I think that there isn't a God, and there is one, then after death I discover I was wrong and, presumably, pay an eternal price for my mistake. On the other hand, if I think that there is a God, and there isn't one, then ... I shall never even know that I was wrong. In other words, Pascal suggested, rather cynically, that the believer wins both ways! And in any case, he insisted that we have to choose.

'But I don't want to choose! Why can't I stay up there on the wall?' Pascal again: picture life as a journey on a ship. We all have to decide where we're going, we all have to choose which ship we will board. Will it be the ship that's bound for oblivion, darkness for ever, where the dead are buried and forgotten, or the ship that's bound for glory? Passengers who choose the first ship get on board and then behave appropriately: plenty of fun while the journey lasts because there's oblivion when the ship docks at the other end. Passengers who look for glory at the end of the journey behave rather differently!

But surely I can decide not to decide? I'll wait and see. Can't I stay on the wall? Can't I delay going on board? Maybe as time goes by I'll be able to make my mind up. 'No good,' says Pascal, 'vous êtes déjà embarqué', 'you have already started the journey'! You have to behave either this way or that way now. Your lifestyle shows your decision. You are already going one way or the other way. To refuse to make a decision is already a decision: a decision against life after death.

This is important. Our decisions today determine what happens tomorrow. And we can't blame anyone else for what happens tomorrow if we have already made tomorrow's events certain. I was saddened a few years ago to be in a hospital, kneeling by the side of a bed where a young woman lay dying of cancer. She had been a very heavy smoker. Now lung cancer had struck and she was at the end of the road. But her relatives blamed God for the tragedy: 'Why did God allow it? A young woman, with a husband, young children?' Yet she had seen her Dad die of cancer, she knew the danger of smoking and still she *chose* to go on. She fixed her own future. Tomorrow is in some measure always fixed because of today.

The importance of the resurrection of Jesus

Well, so much for Pascal's thinking. So why do *I* believe in life after death? In 1 Corinthians 15 Paul is going to deal with the importance of the resurrection, but starts off with the death of Jesus. Plenty of people saw him crucified. The soldiers at Calvary and the centurion who commanded them, saw that he was dead. Pilate made sure that he was dead. A good many saw him buried. And after that he was seen, alive, by well over five hundred people. Paul was writing only twenty or so years after the crucifixion; most of those five hundred people were still alive, available as witnesses (1 Corinthians 15:6). So, for Paul it was certain that death was not the end. There is life after death. There *is* 'resurrection'. This is the history, these are the witnesses: Jesus rose from the dead.

Apparently Paul's preaching was based firmly on his certainty that death was not the end. The resurrection of Jesus and life after death were, for Paul, inextricably linked. Christ didn't rise from the dead? Then *we* won't. Death is the end? Then preaching is a waste of time: 'if Christ has not been raised then our preaching is in vain and your faith is in vain'. In that case there is no Good News and 'you are still in your sins'. But if Christ *did* rise from the dead? Then so will we: 'in fact Christ has been raised from the dead, the first fruits of those who have fallen asleep'. And that is both good news and bad news.

Good news because few of us want to be snuffed out like a candle. Bad news because we have to reckon with a God who is waiting for us at the end of the road, a God who loves me, but also loves all the people I have ever encountered during my lifetime. And he expects me to justify my treatment of them.

Again, if there is life after death, then even a tough life here doesn't matter all that much. For the Christian, comfort here is nothing compared with glory with Jesus! The fact is that following Jesus often means an uncomfortable life. Jesus himself told those who wanted to follow him:

> 'If anyone would come after me, he must deny himself
> and take up his cross daily and follow me.
> For whoever wants to save his life will lose it,
> but whoever loses his life for me will save it.
> What good is it for a man to gain the whole world
> and yet lose or forfeit his very self?'
>
> *Luke 9:23–25*

Paul knew all about that. He had a rough life. But he could bear that because he could see beyond this present life:

> . . . our light and momentary troubles are achieving for us an eternal glory that far outweighs them all.
>
> *2 Corinthians 4:17*

But if there is, in fact, nothing beyond life? Well, Paul is quite clear about that, too:

> If I fought wild beasts in Ephesus for merely human reasons, what have I gained? If the dead are not raised, 'Let us eat and drink, for tomorrow we die.'
>
> *1 Corinthians 15:32*

Surely that makes good sense?

What will we look like?

I still have a question. Everyone knows that when most people die their bodies are destroyed, either buried and left to decay, or reduced to ashes in a crematorium. So my body will eventually disappear. That seems to mean that if 'I' am still alive I will be minus a body – and that I find difficult to imagine. What's more, floating around as a sort of vapour doesn't seem like much of an eternal life.

Paul again: 'But someone will ask, "How are the dead raised? With what kind of body will they come?"' (1 Corinthians 15:35) Christianity believes not merely in life after death, with a spooky kind of vapour instead of a body, but in resurrection. So is my body, buried in a grave or a scattering of ashes, somehow reconstituted? I mean, God could do it, I suppose, but is that what happens?

If God does somehow put the atoms and molecules back together again, there are some more questions. Will it be that same aged body? If so, that's a bit hard on those who die at ninety or so, all right for those who die at twenty, and not so good, again, for those who die as babies. To be an eternal grandaddy ... or an eternal infant. . ? And another thing: over the centuries those atoms and molecules have gone into the construction of dozens, maybe hundreds and thousands of different bodies. Surely there will be hundreds of us all laying claim to the same atoms and molecules? There won't be enough atoms and molecules to go round!

Well, that's not the way Paul explained it. He didn't go for the idea of a vapour in place of a body, and he didn't go for the idea of a body like the one we now have. Paul's view was much more interesting. He saw the future resurrection body as a spiritual body: it would not be the same as the material body we now have, but it would be somehow related to it. He explained that with a truly inspired illustration, the seed and plant:

> What you sow is not the body which is to be, but a bare kernel, perhaps of wheat or of some other grain. But God gives it a body as he has chosen, and to each kind of seed its own body.
>
> *1 Corinthians 15:37–38*

Let me explain how that simple but brilliant illustration came to life for me. When I was living in Ethiopia I discovered that I was not one of nature's great gardeners. But I discovered that I could grow two things: eucalyptus trees and carrots. I grew thousands of both. Eucalyptus trees can easily be grown from seed. The seeds develop inside small, pyramid-shaped nuts. You put the nuts out in the sun, and then when they are dry and begin to open up you shake the seeds out. They are tiny, black, spheres. The ground needs to be carefully prepared, and then you sow the seeds, and cover them over with a very fine layer of soil and a mulching of leaves or grass. Keep it all damp, and soon the seeds begin to sprout. And in five years you have . . . rows of enormous black spheres.

You don't, of course. What you actually get from each of those tiny black spheres is a magnificent tree with shimmering green and silver leaves. Tall, slender, elegant. And that is the body God has prepared for the tiny, black, sphere.

Again, the carrot seeds don't look in the least like tiny carrots. Nor, in fact, do they look like eucalyptus seeds. And for the pale-coloured carrot seeds God has prepared a remarkable, long, brilliant orange body with a feathery cap of green.

Two quite different seeds and two entirely different bodies developing from them. But there is a unique relationship between every seed and every plant that grows from it. Somehow the essence of the eucalyptus tree is there in the seed. No two eucalyptus trees are ever exactly the same, and yet undeniably all are eucalyptus trees; no two carrots are ever exactly the same, but each carrot is uniquely related to its seed:

> So it will be with the resurrection of the dead. The body that is sown is perishable, it is raised imperishable; it is sown in dishonour, it is raised in glory; it is sown in weakness, it is raised in power; it is sown a natural body, it is raised a spiritual body.
>
> *1 Corinthians 15:42–44*

And Paul is absolutely sure about all this: '*If there is a physical body, there is also a spiritual body*'. There certainly is a physical body. I've got one! It is equally certain then that there is a spiritual body. I will have one! And that spiritual body which I will one day have is related to this physical body that I've now got, in the same way as the eucalyptus tree is to the seed from which it grew. Uniquely connected, true; but in almost every conceivable way the spiritual body will be different from the physical body to which it relates. Different.

Do you see how brilliant this illustration is? It doesn't pretend to describe the spiritual body. But it conjures up this marvellous illustration of a handful of passive, dull, uninteresting seeds, and fields of corn gleaming, shimmering in the sun, avenues of magnificent trees, their boughs reaching to the skies, the leaves flashing in the sun like shoals of fish in some blue tropical lagoon.

This present body is so dull compared with the spiritual body which God has prepared for it. As I write this I'm already past the sixty mark, so that my death will be fairly typical: following a pretty long life. My body is already showing signs of wear and tear. In Paul's words it will be 'sown in weakness'. Well, like it or not, I'm not the spry sixteen that I once was.

At London Bible College we have already begun the tradition of hanging pictures of former Principals on the walls. There is an oil painting of Dr Kevan, the first Principal. There are coloured photographs of Gilbert Kirby and Michael Griffiths, the second and third Principals. And I got to thinking recently that I suppose that one day someone might decide to put me in the line. And then I thought: I'd rather like to get a picture of me now, before I get to retirement age, before the wrinkles are too pronounced. Or better still, a picture of me taken, say, ten years ago. All of which means that quite honestly I'd rather not have a miraculously resurrected body just like the one I've got now, preserved from further decay, guaranteed for eternity. I'd truly prefer something rather different.

The fact is that our bodies will be *spiritual* bodies, with spiritual powers and spiritual beauty, but somehow related to the bodies we now have. And that in turn suggests to me that we shall know one another. My new spiritual eyes will be able to discern in your new spiritual body the former physical friend I saw with my old physical eyes. We will know one another. I could recognise my friends when I was here in a weak physical body, and it seems reasonable to suppose that I shall recognise my friends when I have that marvellous new spiritual body. As George MacDonald commented: 'Shall we be greater fools in Paradise than we are here?'!

2 Corinthians chapter 5

The second part of the New Testament that deals with death comes in Paul's *second* letter to the church at Corinth. Actually the subject of death and glory carries through from chapter three verse seven right to the end of chapter five. In chapter three he is talking about just how marvellous (he uses the word 'glory') the New Testament (or New *Covenant*) is, compared with the old one. When Moses received the old covenant at Sinai (the whole story is well worth reading at one sitting, from Exodus 19:1 through to 24:18), it was such a tremendous experience for him and the people that they never forgot it. Moses somehow encountered God. And as a result of that encounter his face *shone*, it reflected the light of that amazing meeting with God up on the mountain. But Christians should shine, too, says Paul: 'we all reflect the Lord's glory', and we are all 'being transformed into his likeness with ever increasing glory, which comes from the Lord' (3:18).

Chapter 4, in the NIV, is headed, 'Treasures in jars of clay.' Now that is helpful. We human beings are far more than walking marvels of evolutionary development. The real marvel is not the body, nor even the brain. After all, the brain is just another part of the material body. You can see it, weigh it, damage it, just as you can the liver or your kidneys. No, the real marvel is the human spirit, the treasure that somehow (and so far no-one has any notion *how*) gives life to the body.

That, incidentally, fits in beautifully with Genesis 2:7, where God forms man from the dust of the earth, but then *breathes into him the breath of life* and so man becomes a living being. It's this mysterious 'me' that animates the body and makes a person, and is the real treasure. And that helps explain death. Death is nothing more than this human soul – this living treasure which actually *animates*, gives life to, the otherwise inanimate flesh – leaving the body. In chapter five Paul uses another inspired illustration: this time of the body as a tent. That's the body I live in now. And as the tent gets older so it becomes more worn. The canvas gets torn and is sewn up. I could show you a good many places on my body which have been sewn up by clever surgeons. The tent poles break. My twin brother has broken his leg twice, but the break was repaired. Nowadays we both know that our bones are even more fragile than they were fifty years back. But although the tent is getting ever more fragile that is not true of the spirit that lives in it. On the contrary what *should* be happening is that as the body gets older and more fragile, so the spirit gets stronger through its experience of the love and presence of God.

And then (5:1) 'if the earthly tent we live in is destroyed, we have a building from God, an eternal house in heaven'. I recall so well the first time I heard these words used in a funeral service. Faith Rayner had come out to Ethiopia as a medical doctor, to work short term in a rather remote part of the country. She came to the end of her time, and went out to the airstrip near the clinic where she had been working, to catch the DC3 flight to Addis Ababa, the first leg of the journey home. She felt unwell, and cancelled her flight, managed to get back to her little house . . . and there she died. They brought her body up to Addis Ababa for the funeral. I shared in the service. And I shall never forget the preacher that day pointing to the coffin at the front of the church:

> Don't imagine that Faith is in that box! No!
> She lived in that body, that tent, for twenty-six years.
> And then the storm came, and the wind blew, and the tent blew down.
> But Faith is all right!
> She stepped out of the tent and into the eternal home.

Out of the tent and into the 'eternal house in heaven, not built by human hands', that house which is in some way related to the present tent. Paul therefore goes on (in verses 2–4) to talk a little bit more about the contrast between the *present* experience of life and what we can expect in the future. He profoundly expresses our fears, our doubts.

Here we are in this world with all its uncertainties, but at least we do *know* what life is like here. And over there is heaven, life beyond death, and that looks pretty wonderful. Here is the tent, and it's getting badly worn. There is the home, and it looks marvellous. But it's getting from the tent into the house that is the problem. The real problem is not so much *death* as *dying*.

So how can we set these fears of ours at rest? How can we lose our fear of the 'dying' bit? The answer is simple: 'It is God who has made us for this very purpose, and has given us the Spirit as a deposit, guaranteeing what is to come' (v 5). Logically, then, cultivating our walk in the Holy Spirit should strengthen our confidence in God, and should enable us to see that he, the Spirit, is the guarantee of all that is to come. At the College a few years back we had a letter from a Trust Fund promising to pay the college £20,000 each year to help students from Eastern Europe to come to the college for study. That letter was my guarantee that the money was there. On the strength of the letter I invited students from Eastern Europe to come to the college and promised that if they would trust me, make the journey, all would be well at this end. And each year I wrote to the Trust Fund asking for the money they had promised, and each year the money came. The letter was the guarantee. So far as the journey through that door called death is concerned, the Spirit is the guarantee. If I have him, and every Christian *does* (Romans 8:9, see also John 14:16), then the heavenly home is certain!

And so Paul concludes this vital chapter about death:

> Therefore we are always confident,
> and know that as long as we are at home in the
> body we are away from the Lord.
> We live by faith, not by sight.
> We are confident, I say,
> and would prefer to be away from the body and at

home with the Lord.
So we make it our goal to please him,
whether we are at home in the body or away from it.
For we must all appear before the judgment seat of
Christ,
that each one may receive what is due to him
for the things done while in the body,
whether good or bad.

2 Corinthians 5:6–10

Chapter Five

DYING AND DEATH

I do not look forward to the prospect of dying, but I do look forward to death itself. It will be a glorious release. It will be the fulfilment of everything I have ever longed for.

Billy Graham

There are just two topics in this chapter: first the experience of being with someone who is dying, and second the question of what to expect after someone has died. I'm writing here for the Christian: but anyone who is *not* a Christian may find what is said relevant and helpful.

The experience of dying

Well, I haven't had that experience of dying, so I can't describe it. But I've been with people as they have been dying. So at least I know 'dying' because I have watched it. The first thing to say is that there is no 'normal' pattern of dying. Both my mother and my mother-in-law died very peacefully. There was no struggle at the last. In fact when my mother died it was difficult to know just when it happened, it was all so very gentle. In contrast, a neighbour in Africa died after being bitten by a rabid dog, and his death was both violent and distressing.

Death is often preceded by quite a long period of unconsciousness, which is sometimes nature's gentle anaesthetic, sometimes the result of injury to the brain. But sometimes the one who is dying knows exactly what is happening and may even welcome the knowledge, 'I'm going home'! And very often it seems as though towards the end of the road our experiences may become more intense, more real, than ever before:

> ... the consciousness of the dying person by no means becomes feebler and feebler, like a dying candle. Nor does it merely flicker up again, like a candle just before it goes out. On the contrary it undergoes an unheard of intensification, such as it had hardly ever experienced in life.
>
> (*Hampe, 1979, p 78*)

The old Victorian melodrama written around death is very rarely seen: a halo of light, a happy smile, a vision of angels, the sound of a heavenly choir. Not that it *never* happens. Leslie Weatherhead, that great Methodist preacher, told of a man who was dying, and Dr Weatherhead was holding his hand ... perhaps too firmly. The man called out, weakly, but clearly, 'Don't hold me back! I can see through the gates ... it's marvellous' (Leslie Weatherhead, *Life Begins at Death*, p 16).

I know that when people discover they are dying they respond differently. I remember going to visit a lady who had been taken into hospital after a long period of illness, because her relatives could no longer give her the necessary care. The end of the road was very near, just a few days away, in fact. And yet she said to me, with some vigour, 'I don't know why they've brought me here'. Now she almost certainly *did* know why she had been brought to the hospital, but she just didn't want to accept the knowledge. So there's the response of denial. Sometimes there's the response of fear. We had my wife's mother with us for the last few months of her life, and at one point she told me that she was frightened. I suppose that my response would be dismissed by some people as being superficial, but what I said was:

'Why are you afraid? You love Jesus. Jesus loves you!'

There was silence for a moment as she thought over what I'd said. Then:

'Yes! I love Jesus, and Jesus loves me!'

and I did not hear her mention fear again.

But the fear of death isn't always taken away that easily. For some people death and dying are subjects they have never talked about, never read about. The thought of death has been shut away, and now that it can be shut away no longer they simply don't know enough about it to be able to face it with a sense of peace. Instead there is a sense of panic, of fear. If that sense of fear is present then it is always going to be right to get it out into the open, to discuss the fear, to talk about dying and death. But it is vital that if *you* are going to talk about it then you should take time to learn about it so that you will be able to answer the obvious questions. Other people fear death because of uncertainties about their loved ones whom they must leave behind. It is very important that we should do everything possible to ensure that husbands, wives, children will be properly cared for. Here is a great opportunity for the church to show that it really is a caring community, and not merely a Sunday congregation!

Still others fear death because of wrongs done by them and not put right. Two things can be said here. First the dying should be helped to confess; to admit to someone else, to a friend, to a minister, the wrongs that have been kept hidden away, the sins that have spoiled the past.

Second, we should work with the dying to help them to put wrongs right: to be reconciled with relatives.

It is almost always the case that people who are dying like to have people with them. There is a certain fear of dying alone, of there being no-one there at that last, unique moment. Relatives should be aware of this need for company, and should then try to ensure that visitors come regularly – the right kind of visitors and the right number. Few people who are really ill can cope with a crowd of people chattering like so many magpies. And it's difficult for anyone to cope with visitors who are over emotional and even melodramatic about death. I recall with pleasure, now, the last morning that I spent with my mother. I had been called by the hospital with the news that she had had a bad night, had been given oxygen, but that her condition was very serious. So I went in to the room where she was lying. She told me about the rough night she had had, and about what the nurses had done to help her, and about the oxygen. Actually neither of us knew just how close the end of the road was, and perhaps that helped. We talked about the old days, what we'd done, where we'd been. I got one thing cleared up:

'Which day of the week was I born on?'

She thought carefully, and then, quite definitely,

'Sunday.'

I think that she had gone back in her thinking to the military hospital at Imtarfa, in Malta, where Cliff and I were born, and recalled just what had happened. . . We smiled about that 'Sunday'. We joined in the bit of doggerel:

Monday's child is fair of face
Tuesday's child is full of grace,
Wednesday's child is kind and willing,
Thursday's child works hard for a living
Friday's child is full of woe
Saturday's child has far to go,
But the child that is born on the sabbath day
    is good and kind and strong and gay.

And then we prayed together. The last thing we ever did together on this earth. That *is* a very good memory. Talking over the past is very satisfying for everyone involved. For Christians, prayer is the great comfort.

There is a common experience connected with those who are dying, that relatives may have to face. Sometimes the dying person is unconscious and may be unconscious for days or even weeks. I recall sitting for some time each day for six weeks with a friend of mine who eventually died without ever regaining consciousness. And there I had occasional confirmation of what I had once been told, that the faculty of *hearing* is one of the last to be lost. I sat there, sometimes alone, sometimes with his wife, sometimes with several others. We talked together and we prayed together. And just sometimes I saw a faint smile on his face, sometimes I felt a weak pressure from his hand, in response to a joke, a comment, a prayer. So even in the presence of someone who is apparently unconscious: no levity, nothing unkind. That is inappropriate in the very presence of the eternal.

Where death is delayed there can be a very different problem. We may well feel guilty for wishing that the whole thing was over. The thought is almost, 'Why doesn't he get on and die?' Jenifer Pardoe describes it exactly:

> Physically and emotionally exhausted groups of people sit round the bed of the ill person feeling quite

unable to leave even though they may have children at home or jobs to go to or a multitude of other functions. The vigil becomes such a powerful trap that they cannot break free from it. Conversation dries up, strain and tension increases and relatives will say that they know that the only thing that can break this living and extended nightmare is the death of the person whose bed they are sitting round, but 'what a dreadful thought to have'.

(*Pardoe, 1991, p 52*)

Should the dying person be told?

Is it right to tell someone that they are dying? Here I can't give a simple answer. The fact is that some people, even some Christians, can't cope with that knowledge. Their response to the fact is denial. They don't wish to have that knowledge, perhaps because they know that they can't cope with it. A Christian doctor once told me how she was with the specialist on his rounds in the hospital where she was working as an intern. One patient was very seriously ill with cancer. The little group of doctors clustered round the bed, the specialist made one or two comments, then they moved on. The Christian doctor lingered behind, to share something with the patient that could be a little less impersonal, something with a little warmth in it. The man in the bed suddenly blurted it out: 'It's cancer, isn't it?' He hadn't even been told what he was suffering from. But undoubtedly it *was* cancer. The doctor was caught. She hadn't expected to be asked that question. She was unprepared. 'Yes.' And from there on the patient simply went to pieces. He couldn't cope with the knowledge. And it's no use saying that people *should* be able to cope. The fact is that some people *can't*.

But generally speaking it seems to me that people should be given that knowledge, so that they can make any final arrangements for their families and, even more importantly, sort things out with God. Plenty of people have been reconciled to God right at the end of things. It's never too late!

Death

Then what is death itself? It is a doorway through which we all pass. It is the doorway between two worlds. For most people, on this side of the doorway there is pain and weakness and loneliness, and on that side of the doorway there is love and comfort . . . and, of course, God. For the Christian there is no in-between waiting room. To depart is to be with Christ, and, of course, that is far better.

We are often at fault here. We imagine that those who have died are somewhere or other, maybe still in that grave, *waiting* for the resurrection. Well they aren't. If I may be allowed to be philosophical at this point, it is quite obvious that once we have stepped out of this world we are out of time and into eternity. So there is no sense at all in which the dead are 'waiting'. They are in a permanent 'now' which we certainly can't understand because all we have ever known is time.

Death is a doorway. And you go through it. But what is this 'you'? Well, it is *not* your body (that remains here, and in one sense it no more matters to you than does the house or flat or hospital from which you stepped into eternity). Nor is it your brain. Don't confuse the *brain* with *you*. *You* use your brain. And the death of your brain is not the end of you, any more than the loss of your violin means that you will never play again. Let's suppose that you have a violin, and you learn to play quite well. And then one day someone smashes that violin beyond all hope of repair. But then you are given not just a violin, but a Stradivarius, the work of *the* master craftsman of violins. *Now* you can *really* play! Well, that's a picture of death. Out of this world and into a better. Out of this body and on with a better.

Chapter Six

GRIEF: IT'S OK

I ask: can paradise be restored? Is there light at the end of the tunnel? Or, as the late Winston Churchill asked a young American clergyman nearly thirty years ago, 'Young man, can you give me any hope?'

Billy Graham

I've already mentioned some of my experiences in Ethiopia. In most things I greatly admired the Ethiopian Christians, and most of what I know about the Christian life I learned from them. But I suspect that they had one thing wrong. They didn't allow weeping at the funeral of a Christian.

A mistaken view: no tears

The reason for this rather odd rule is clear enough. The rest of the people of Ethiopia were terrified of death, and had no expectation of a *heaven* to which they might go. Life after death was a mystery, a frightening mystery. The dead weren't *dead*. They hadn't ceased to exist. But now they were in some terrifying way *powerful*, disembodied spirits that were loaded with what the anthropologists call *mana*, a kind of supernatural power that made the spirits of the dead *tabu*, forbidden, different. They lived a shadowy sort of life, vengeful if they felt neglected, unpredictable, implacable, mysterious. But certainly not in any delightful, marvellous, refreshing heaven. And so the people were afraid of death. Death could strike at will. Anyone might be marked down as the next to die. And when anyone died there were the most extravagant expressions of grief and fear. It all seemed to be an attempt to let the spirits see the misery of those poor helpless human beings, to see their fear, and perhaps to have pity on them, to spare them from more death.

For the Christians here was, perhaps, the most important difference that their new faith had made to their lives: they were no longer afraid to die. Beyond the gateway of death there waited a beauty, a happiness that they had never known on earth. Life here was hard and uncertain. Here they must live by faith, unable to *see* the glory of God. But one day it would all be exchanged for the glories of heaven. To die was to be rid of the rags they had known, to end the perennial hunger and to find satisfaction in a new body which would never know hunger or thirst. Illness and tiredness, old age and all its attendant indignities, all gone and instead: heaven! So why weep?

It became a rule. No, not a rule made by unfeeling and imperialistic missionaries, but a rule made by thinking, feeling, concerned, spiritual leaders of the church: no weeping at the funeral of a Christian. Here was the great opportunity to show our neighbours the difference that Christianity makes, to show that death has been defeated. Let the Christian funeral be different. Not *rejoicing*, but certainly not crying. Let there be solemnity in the face of death, let there be dignity, let there be proclamation of the Good News about Jesus. But no weeping.

And there was no weeping.

The emotion we must not deny

But I'm not sure that they had it quite right. All that they had to say about our expectations of heaven was right and so often it truly *is* wonderful when a Christian dies after a long and satisfying life. But the end of the road sometimes comes suddenly, an intrusion, cutting off the life of a child, of a young mother, of a man whose life has begun with great promise that must now remain unfulfilled.

Early one morning in the Ogaden, that fiercely hot, dry, featureless desert area of eastern Ethiopia inhabited by the Somali people, a small group of our missionaries were preparing for their day's work. They were a medical team, working in an area where there was no normal medical care at all. A young Australian doctor led a small team of nurses. He was a short-term volunteer. He set about putting up the tent which would be used as an operating theatre. He probably never even felt the knife that was plunged into his back by a Somali Muslim. He died instantly.

The nurses had the task of striking camp, loading his body into their Land Rover, and driving up to Addis Ababa. I was asked to conduct the funeral service. A couple of hours before the service was due to begin I went to the chapel to make sure that everything was ready. And there I found one of those nurses, huddled in one of the seats, her face streaked with tears, sobbing, shaking with grief: 'It doesn't make sense. . .' She wasn't wrong to cry. There *is* a time to weep.

Again and again I've gone back to that marvellous piece of English history recorded in Bede's *Ecclesiastical History.* He tells how King Edwin of Northumbria was considering whether he should allow Christianity to be preached in his kingdom, or whether this new teaching was to be resisted. He called in his advisers and at a great meeting it was one of them who said to him:

The present life of man on earth, O king, seems to me, in comparison with that time which is unknown to us, like the swift flight of a sparrow. It is as though you were seated in your castle with your Ealdormen and thegns, in winter. Within, the fire blazes, and in the midst the hall is warmed, but without the wintry storms of rain or snow rage, the sparrow, flying in at one door and immediately out at another. Whilst he is within he is safe from the tempest, but after a short space of fair weather he immediately vanishes out of sight, passing *from* winter back into winter again. So this life of man appears for a little while, but of what is to follow, or what went before we know nothing at all. If, therefore, this new teaching tells us something more certain, it seems justly to deserve being followed.

King Edwin followed the advice, and in 627 he was himself baptised as a Christian. And yet in one fundamental respect the old man's advice was mistaken. He had the story the wrong way round. In fact *the storm is inside the castle*. Here we sit around the fire, muffled up against the storms of life which rage all about us. And yet outside the sky is blue, the weather is warm, the air is refreshing. *The storm is in the castle!* And that is why we can face death calmly.

So why should we cry at all? What place is there for grief? What should our response to death be? Well, it does depend on the circumstances. Yet even when we are confronted with some horrific tragedy where grief is entirely appropriate, still, our grief must be different. To use Paul's words:

... we do not want you to be ignorant about those who fall asleep, or to grieve like the rest of men, who have no hope. We believe that Jesus died and rose again and so we believe that God will bring with Jesus those who have fallen asleep in him.

1 Thessalonians 4:13–14

So there is this difference: we do not grieve helplessly nor ignorantly. Our grief is tempered by this certainty: death is not the end. Those we have loved are still alive; they are *more* alive! And we shall meet again.

But I feel that I should add a brief note of warning to those people who feel that it is actually *wrong* to show their grief, wrong to cry. God has given to us emotions – anger, joy, sorrow, fear. And each one of those emotions has been given to us for a reason; we stifle them at our peril. When we do manage to stifle these God-given emotions we become less human, even *inhuman*. And we do damage to ourselves. So if you have suffered bereavement recently but you have fiercely stemmed up the emotions, held back the tears, let me say very gently: it's OK to cry. It could be harmful not to cry.

Some while back there was a young family living in London: husband and wife, two boisterous, healthy lads, and a third child on the way. Jenny (not her real name) had to go to the hospital for a regular pre-natal check so John agreed to look after the boys that morning. Jenny had her check-up and all was well. She came out of the hospital, crossed the road and suddenly . . . a screaming of brakes, a terrible accident, and Jenny and her unborn baby died instantly. John phoned me to let me know what had happened. But he had somehow picked up the idea that real Christians, Christians with a deep faith, didn't grieve. Everything was actually planned by God, so how could we be sad when God had planned things for us? He kept up this strange, unreal, response for several weeks. It wasn't a denial of the death: he took the boys to see their mother's body. But he denied the *tragedy*. It was wonderful! It was the goodness of God! God was in control! At the funeral he insisted on taking part, with a disjointed and incongruous 'testimony'. A month later came a total nervous breakdown.

I don't know where John got that theology. It was not a Christian theology. We must take seriously the Christian understanding of a fallen world and of a Second Kingdom. We recognise that it is *not* God's will for aircraft to be bombed out of the sky, for war victims to be raped and plundered, for Catholics and Protestants to be murdered. It is *right* for us to mourn and grieve over our experience of a tragic, marred, fallen, world.

David knew all about that fallen world. He was king and his own son, Absalom, set up a rebellion to overthrow him. But the rebellion failed and Absalom was killed. When they came to give David the news of Absalom,

> ... the king was deeply moved, and went up to the chamber over the gate, and wept; and as he went, he said. 'O my son Absalom, my son, my son Absalom! Would I had died instead of you, O Absalom, my son, my son!'
>
> *2 Samuel 18:33* RSV

It's OK to grieve.

Anger: an unexpected response

There is another response to death: anger. Many people who have been bereaved find it difficult to admit this particular reaction. Somehow we feel that *anger* is a wrong response to death. It seems so irrational.

My father died when I was just a baby of five weeks. He died in Malta, where he was stationed with the Royal Air Force. He was a comparatively young man. Obviously gifted, he had made his way through the ranks and had just been promoted to Warrant Officer. Commissioned rank was not far away, and a long career beyond. He had a beautiful wife who was full of energy; they enjoyed swimming, tennis . . . a good life stretched ahead for them both. They already had one son, now twin boys. And then illness struck: appendicitis followed by peritonitis, and death.

My mother brought us all back to England. She married again, and she very rarely talked to us about our father. We knew that he had died in Malta. We had even caught glimpses of some photographs of the military funeral and of the cemetery where his body had been laid. After our mother died, Clifford, my twin brother, and I decided to go out to Malta to find the grave where our father was buried. We located the cemetery and, on the last day of our week in Malta, we stood together by the grave. He lay in a shady cemetery near the city of Medina, in clear view of the hospital where Clifford and I had been born. The cemetery was beautifully cared for by the Imperial War Graves Commission. But as I stood there I was conscious not particularly of *sorrow*. It was *anger* that I felt. And the emotion troubled me. Surely tears would be right, but not this *anger*?

But then I remembered a commentary on John's Gospel that I had read many years ago. It was written by Professor C K Barrett then of Durham University. I remembered he had insisted that in John chapter 11 – the account of the miraculous raising of Lazarus to life – when Jesus saw the tears of Mary and the others, *he was not merely 'deeply moved' but was actually 'angry'*.

When eventually we got back home I found my copy of Barrett's commentary (published by SPCK, second edition 1967, p 399) and sure enough, there it was: 'It is beyond question that *enebrimesato* (the Greek verb used in John 11:33) implies anger'. Later on I came across Professor George Beasley-Murray's commentary on John's Gospel and was very much struck by his explanation of Jesus' *anger*:

> What was the cause of his anger? Verse 33 makes it plain: 'When Jesus saw her weeping, and the Jews who came out with her weeping. . .' They sorrowed, as Paul put it, 'like the rest of men, who have no hope' (1 Thessalonians 4:13), which is irreconcilable with faith in the resurrection.
>
> *(Beasley-Murray, 1987, p 193)*

His anger was because of their *hopelessness*, because of their lack of faith. They just didn't believe that death was a gateway to heaven. Probably no-one had put it that way to them. The religious leaders of the day didn't really give the people a living hope. And Jesus was angry because of their hopelessness.

Well, that's part of the answer. But my anger had another element to it, and I think that the anger of Jesus had another part to it as well. Jesus was deeply moved by the tears of Mary and her friends. He could see death as we see it, as the last enemy, as an intrusion into life, as something that breaks our relationships, breaks our hearts. He could see it as something that God never intended for us, the consequence of sin getting into the world.

I felt robbed. I just don't know what life might have been like if only my father had lived. The simple fact is that like so many millions of others I never knew the love of my father. My stepfather did his best. Indeed as a boy I always thought of him as my father. I know now that he had real difficulty in seeing us as his boys. And now I know that actually I missed out on that unique relationship between a boy and his father. Death robbed me, and I was angry. Not angry with God. Not at all! But angry with sin which has brought so much pain into the world, pain far greater than the pain I felt there beside a grave in Malta.

71

The pain of all those killed in wars, of the millions who have died in famine, of those who have died of cancer, of AIDS, of all the other diseases, the pain of the deaths of little children.

So there are two biblical responses to death: there is biblical grief, which is softened by the certainty of resurrection, the knowledge that after all death is not the end. And there is anger, an anger that recognises that this kind of death is not what God wanted. It is an alien intrusion. It came into the world along with sin.

So grief is all right, sorrow is in order, even anger may be right. But both sorrow and anger need to follow the biblical patterns of sorrow and anger. We need help when we pass through this experience of bereavement. Perhaps what we need more than anything else, is the chance to talk about our loss. And that's where our society tends to let us down. Such talk is so often discouraged. Friends and family will talk about anything else, but to talk about the one we have lost is often thought to be morbid. Well, I don't think so. It is good to be able to recall good times and bad times, to get it all out, to talk it all through, with people who will understand.

Obviously, when someone we know dies our grief is determined by just how close our relationship was. A happily married couple will find it almost impossible, to imagine life without each other. A divorced or separated couple might imagine that the death of the partner will make very little impact. But actually the death of anyone in any way related to us *hurts*, because death is always the closing of a door, the end of an opportunity of *reliving* experiences which only we shared, and of mending broken or spoiled relationships. And it seems as though the more experiences we shared, the harder it is to lose the relationship. But in some sense *every* death leaves me poorer:

Any man's death diminishes me,
because I am involved in mankind;
and therefore never send to know for whom the bell
tolls;
it tolls for thee.

(John Donne)

It is a strange experience to *expect* someone's death, to be *prepared* for it, to assure oneself that it is inevitable, that it is natural, and that it may even be a relief. I thought all of that before my mother died. She was over eighty years old. She was frail, yet still able to care for herself and she was not in pain. As she lived not too far from me, I was able to see her each day. And I assured myself that I was prepared for the inevitable time when she would be taken away from me. I wasn't. It took a year before I could really feel that I was over the pain of the separation.

Seven stages of grief

When we lose someone who is very close to us, very special, we sincerely wonder if we will ever recover from our loss, ever get back to the experience of what we remember as 'normal' living. We tend to pass through a whole set of reactions. Not everyone goes through the same set, and some have quite different reactions, but there is always a progression of some kind.

Denial, shock, numbness. The three are so closely connected but the result is a refusal to believe the fact: death is simply dismissed, discounted, disallowed. This is particularly true of any sudden or particularly tragic death. We can't take it in. We know that we can't cope, and the safest reaction is to deny that it has happened.

Strongly religious people may even invoke a miracle to reverse the death. The son of a missionary died, totally unexpectedly. The boy's father announced to everyone that the boy was simply sleeping, that although this was 'death' of a kind, it was really sleeping, and Jesus would come and perform a miracle, like the miracle performed for that daughter of Jairus (Luke 8:40–56). Their son would miraculously rise from the dead. But he didn't. And the result was that they were never able to talk about their dead son as other bereaved parents could. His death represented failure on someone's part: his, theirs, God's?

Sometimes the denial stage is less bizarre. The desk is left exactly as he left it. The furniture, the curtains, must not be changed. Her clothes can't be disposed of. His garden tools must not be used by anyone else. And lurking in the background is the unspoken belief that she might need them again. Of course this is not at all the same as holding on to precious mementoes of the one who died. That is *quite* a different matter, and entirely healthy.

We may find ourselves searching the faces of the people we meet in the street, expecting, hoping to find the one we have lost out there, to discover that the whole thing has been one great big misunderstanding: he is alive!

Anger. Sooner or later we may feel angry with God, whom we had supposed to be in charge and who should have prevented this happening. Surprisingly the anger is sometimes directed at the person who has died. 'How could he do this to me? I'm left to manage all by myself!' 'We were just in the middle of getting the house sorted out and he dies!' Or the anger may be turned against someone else, anyone else, for the slightest reason, and even for no obvious reason at all. And then, whether we are angry with God or angry with the one who has died or angry with someone else, we feel guilty just because we are angry. Then we may attempt to deny that we *are* angry, instead of admitting it, and recognising that anger is very often a normal part of the grief process. And that is sad, because what is important in the whole grief process is *honesty*. Let me be honest with myself: *I am angry.* So let me still be honest: *Why am I angry?* And then I can gradually deal with the anger.

Yearning and searching. A possible third stage is related to the denial stage, but shows progress beyond denial. I must admit that he has died but still there is a yearning for the one who has died, accompanied by an anguished restlessness, and then physical exhaustion. And the thought, 'He is still here with me. Of course I know that he isn't *dead*. Jesus himself said "Whoever lives and believes in me shall never die." His body is dead, but he is wonderfully alive. In fact, more alive than ever. I sense his presence right here, in this room.' Well, there is a measure of truth in what is being said, but the Christian does *not* believe that the dead are here, around us, in some personal, almost tangible way. It is the angels who are the divine messengers, not the spirits of God's redeemed people. The soul of my husband is not hovering around me here in my home, nor shall I encounter him through a visit to his grave. He is not there. He is not here. He is with Christ, which is *better by far* (Philippians 1:23).

Anxiety and hyper-activity. The fourth stage may well be a stage of anxiety and hyper-activity. House cleaning. Gardening. Visiting. Working late. Overtime. Writing long letters. Up early in the morning. Late to bed at night and, in between, ceaseless activity. To be healthily tired when one has been bereaved is very desirable, because most of us find it very difficult to get off to sleep otherwise. So activity is better than total inertia. But hyper-activity actually leads to sleeplessness, and that in turn may lead to more activity, and eventually total exhaustion.

Guilt. The fifth stage may be a stage of feeling guilty. Guilt takes so many different forms. I feel guilty because I am alive. I feel guilty because if I had acted differently it might have made a difference to you. If only I had allowed you to drive! If only I hadn't gone out to church that evening. If only I had watched you more carefully. If only

I had thought! If only. . .

> My name is Might-have-been;
> I am also called No-more, Too-late, Farewell.
>
> (*Dante Gabriel Rossetti*)

And we know it! But we blame ourselves even when we know that it *wouldn't* have made a difference, still more when we think that it *could* have made a difference. But most of all because we know that now it *can't* make a difference. Let me simply say that it's best to get the might-have-been out into the open, to allow it to be considered and thought through, so that when you are ready it can be discarded.

It's not always the big things that we feel guilty about. It can be something quite small, like the guilt I felt when my grandmother died. My brother and I used to cycle over to see her on Sunday afternoons. It was quite a long way, several miles, and that particular Sunday we just didn't go. That week she died, and at once there was that guilty feeling: 'If only I'd gone!'

Depression. Grief can become deepened to despair: the feeling that life is no longer worth living. That's not surprising when bereavement is so long a process, with so much pain and emotional turmoil. The feeling of despair often accompanies the ending of a particularly close relationship: husband or wife, parent or child. And the more unexpected or tragic the circumstances, so the deeper the sense of despair. And we do feel in such circumstances that life can never be meaningful again. It's no use telling us that time is the great healer. It may be true for others, but for myself I can't believe it. Now is the time for my friends, my church, to come round me and hold me, and show me that there are other loves waiting for me, loves that can never be a substitute for the love I have lost, but love for all that.

Acceptance and healing. Grief can be therapeutic: it has healing powers. Tear ducts were given to us for more than lubricating the eyes: tears help us to healing. But grief doesn't need to be forced, it can wait for its proper time. I remember my brother saying to me as we stood together by the side of our mother when she died, 'Go on, Peter, let it go', but I couldn't. Not then. I hadn't got there yet. But the time came for grief, and then I cried.

And so the perfect seven lead me forward to the time when I can quietly think back over the life of the one I have lost, talk about her without the danger of tears. That time will come, if I will allow it to come. After how long? Well, I just don't know. It is different for every one of us, for every experience of bereavement. It may take years. But it will come.

Chapter Seven

ABOUT FUNERALS

Death casts its shadow over the land . . .

Billy Graham

I must admit that arranging a funeral in Africa was so much easier than it is back here in the western world. We had no undertakers to 'undertake', to take over responsibility. Instead we were free to arrange what we felt to be appropriate. Many people I've talked with about funerals have agreed that the usual funeral is not *really* satisfyingly *Christian*.

What funerals are expected to do

What is the purpose of a funeral? First, *the funeral is a means of reverently disposing of the body of the one who has died*. It is surely important to remember right through the planning and carrying out of a funeral that it is a *body* that we are dealing with. The energising, life-giving spirit is not there to *be* buried. The spirit has gone, and that is why we can talk about *death*. The spirit gives life to the body: remove the spirit and the body dies. But we ought really to avoid talking about Jack's burial, or Jack's grave. We *can* talk about a thanksgiving service for Jack's life. What you can't do is to bury *Jack*.

But Jack lived in that body for a good many years. The

body itself is a marvellous part of God's creation, holding within it some part of the looks and characteristics of mother and father, of grandmother and grandfather, and so on back indefinitely, through hundreds of years. Gradually, through the study of the biologists, through the patient decoding of the DNA chains, we are coming to a very basic understanding of how this process of transmission works. But it is amazing. And because it *is* amazing, and because this body has been not merely the location of an infinite stretch of human history but also the home of a unique individual, and because God *made* it, it is to be *reverently* disposed of.

Throughout history mankind everywhere has observed that principle. Human bodies are not simply thrown out and left to decay. Some formal way is chosen to dispose of them.

Second, a funeral is *an opportunity for those who are left behind to acknowledge the break, to say farewell.* Many of us find this extremely difficult to do. There is a danger of holding on to the past, of denying the reality of death and trying to carry on as though the one who has died is still with us. As a small boy I remember seeing the great actress Anna Neagle playing Queen Victoria in 'Sixty Glorious Years'. And even though I was only six or seven years old I was deeply affected by the portrayal of Victoria as a widow, following the death of her beloved husband Bertie. What a strange, uncharacteristic, unexpected love-story that had been. Victoria seemed to be a rather typical, prosaic, German *Hausfrau*, elevated to the role of Queen-Empress, perpetually 'not-amused'. But then came Bertie, and life was wonderful. When tragically he died she said of him, 'He was such a one as I would gladly have walked around the world barefooted with.' And maybe the preposition at the end of the sentence is the best indication of the deep sincerity of the otherwise pedantic Queen. The film introduced a scene from Queen Victoria's retreat,

'Osborne', on the Isle of Wight. It is time for afternoon tea. The table is laid and Queen Victoria, in deep mourning, sweeps into the room, to be helped to her seat by a servant. 'Thank you', she says, with enormous dignity (I can hear Anna Neagle's words now, as I write after all these years), 'I will pour tea myself.' And she begins to do so. Two cups. She simply couldn't let Bertie go.

Maybe an extreme example, but many people find it so difficult to let go of the past. His suits are carefully kept and regularly cleaned, as though he might come at any moment to demand one of them. Her wardrobe is left exactly as it was in her lifetime, as though she might need to choose a dress for some special occasion. The furniture cannot be removed, the decoration cannot be changed, the daily schedule remains the same. 'And what of the dead person's belongings, objects that mattered to him, objects from his earlier past? It seems to me a denial of his existence to dispose of them or lock them away.' (Elspeth Baker, 'The Longest Goodbye', *The Guardian*, October 19, 1992). We can all understand that. But eventually we must let go.

A funeral ought to be the occasion when we say farewell, when we begin to accept our loss, when we admit that a new chapter of life must begin.

Third, a funeral is *a marvellous opportunity for thanking God for what he was able to do in the life of the one who has died*. So the term 'service of thanksgiving' is entirely appropriate. There is, of course, a danger here, that a service of thanks to God for all that he has done should be turned into an unreal service of praise to the one who has died. It is often so embarrassing to listen to that kind of eulogy, where you really can scarcely recognise in what the speaker is saying the person you knew. It seems now that he was the paragon of all the virtues: never lost his temper, always in church, friends everywhere, beloved by all. Where are the warts?

I conducted a funeral service once for a lady who had really been quite an awkward sort of person. She had been snappy, critical. Towards the end of her life she began to realise just how snappy and critical she had been, and realised, too, that this could explain why her husband and her children had not followed her way. They had little to do with the church. And she was deeply sorry. Of course the husband and sons were all there at the funeral service. I referred to what she had been saying to me in the days before her death. The husband told me, later, how the family had talked about that especially after the service. They were surprised that I should know the old lady so well, and very touched by the discovery that she didn't imagine that she was perfect, that she had wanted to do better and that she was truly sorry that she had failed so often.

Fourth, the funeral service is *an opportunity for bringing comfort to the bereaved*, to share with them the God of all comfort, the one who offers comfort to everyone in every conceivable situation. Christianity is in many ways different from other religions, but it is particularly different because we believe in a triune God: Father, Son and Holy Spirit, in some way each equally God. And so when Christ came into this world it was God stepping into the world, setting aside his glory, as Paul explains in Philippians 2, and experiencing what we experience. So God saw the tears of that woman from the village of Nain, whose husband had died and whose son had now died: 'the only son of his mother, and she was a widow' (Luke 7:12). Luke describes the scene very movingly: 'When the Lord saw her, his heart went out to her and he said "Don't cry." ' At the grave of Lazarus Jesus wept (John 11:35). God doesn't just identify with our tears from a distance, pretending that he understands. He was here. He shared in the experience of grief. And so he is fitted to be the God of all comfort (2 Corinthians 1:3).

Burial or cremation?

Some Christians feel very strongly that burial is the proper *Christian* and *biblical* way of disposing of the body, and may even feel that cremation is wrong. The first thing to be said here is that we must respect other people's views, and not criticise those who happen to disagree with us on such issues. Of course, real problems arise when some relatives are content with cremation and others insist on burial. The end result can be a great deal of bad feeling at a time when everybody is understandably sensitive.

Let's deal with one criticism of cremation first, that it is an attempt to escape the resurrection. It is certainly the case that when George Bernard Shaw set down in his will that his body was to be cremated he felt that he was shaking his fist at God and mocking the Christian idea of the resurrection of the body: 'Now resurrect *that*!' But many fine Christians have asked that their bodies should be cremated rather than buried. In 1944 Dr William Temple was the first Archbishop of Canterbury to be cremated, and amongst others to choose this way of disposal of the body were Dr W E Sangster and Dr Campbell Morgan: they certainly weren't trying to escape the resurrection!

Let me say next that *burial* in a coffin which is then placed in the ground, and the earth put back over it has been the traditional *British* way of burial for *ordinary* people for many centuries. But it is by no means the only way: most churchyards have examples of above-ground family vaults, with places for several coffins; vaults which can be opened from time to time for further family interments. And churches often have similar facilities within the buildings themselves.

Some people will argue that they think that we should follow the 'biblical' practice. But of course, in the main we don't. In the Bible we have examples of burial in a cave. Abraham bought a cave specifically as a burial place for his wife Sarah (Genesis chapter 23 gives quite a detailed account of the transaction). And when Jesus died on the cross his body was not buried in the ground, but similarly in a cave, with a stone to seal the entrance to it. So actually burial in the ground is not particularly a biblical practice although it certainly is not *unbiblical*!

Cremation is different. It was *not* the normal way of disposing of a body in Old Testament Israel, although there are four references to bodies being burned. But they don't really help us in deciding whether *cremation* is right or wrong. The first mention is in Amos 2:1–3. Moab is condemned because the Moabites disinterred the body of the king of Moab and then burned it: a malicious action intended to dishonour him. It is even possible that they burned his body as a sacrifice to their gods. Judges 15:6 probably means no more than that the Philistines burned down the house where Samson's wife and her father lived, and they died in the fire. The third example concerns Achan, and is recorded in Joshua chapter 7. He had broken the *herem*, the absolute ban placed on everything in the town of Jericho. He looted gold and silver, and a rich robe that he probably used to carry it all in, and then buried everything in his tent floor. Joshua ordered everything connected with the incident to be burned, and the place to be marked with a huge cairn of stones. But of course that cannot be seen as in any way parallel to the modern practice of cremation!

And fourth, there is the perplexing account of the burning of the bodies of Saul and his sons, described in 1 Samuel chapter 31. The account begins with the suicide of Saul and the little group that was with him. The bodies were then discovered by the Philistines, who stripped off Saul's armour, cut off his head and nailed up his body on a wall, a most appalling outrage. The people of Jabesh Gilead then determined to end this dreadful scene, attacked Beth Shan, retrieved the bodies and fled with them. Most translations of the Bible then say that when they get back to Jabesh they *burned* the bodies, and later *buried* the bones. Which doesn't make much sense. If they were going to *bury* them there was no need to *burn* them. But now it appears that the Hebrew word that is translated 'burn' can also mean 'anoint', and then the passage makes perfectly good sense. The bodies had not been given the traditional anointing, so that was rectified before the burial: and that's how the New English Bible translates it.

So the Old Testament doesn't really help us in deciding whether cremation is an acceptable way of reverently disposing of the body, although it was not, in fact, a practice of Israel in the Old Testament or of Christians in the New Testament. On the other hand there is no verse that either tells us how a Christian funeral *should* be arranged, nor any verse that tells us how it *should not* be arranged.

If we look at our own culture, it is very clear that our practice has changed over the past thirty or so years. Cremation is now much more common than it used to be; about sixty percent of funerals today involve cremation. The shift is probably largely for practical reasons: the process of urbanisation, people moving to the cities and the growth in population, means that cemeteries have been getting too big.

And to be very practical it has to be said that the cremation service is less expensive than the traditional burial service, and that it is generally much easier on the bereaved. The chapel of the crematorium is usually comparatively modern and carefully designed so that a sense of community is produced. So many churches are simply too big for an age in which it is almost impossible for anyone other than close relatives to get time off work to attend a funeral. And it is also true that the graveside service is almost always difficult and the grave itself intimidating.

If cremation is decided on, then a decision has to be taken regarding the disposal of the ashes, which may be reverently interred in the grounds of the crematorium or, less commonly, taken elsewhere, for example to the grave of a beloved relative, for interment.

Perhaps it is worth adding here that the funeral service is meant to provide the necessary acceptance of the finality of death. The service at the graveside is very definite at this point: there is the coffin, which is placed in the grave, and the grave is filled in. The relatives walk away. The finality is very clear. The service at a crematorium may be less definite. There seem to be three ways of closing the service. At the Committal, the coffin is taken through curtains or doors and so out of the chapel and the relatives will not see it again. Secondly curtains may be drawn across the bier holding the coffin, so that it can no longer be seen by the relatives. Or thirdly the words of the committal are spoken, and the congregation leaves the chapel, but the coffin is still in full view. I have put these three in what I believe to be the order of preference, and you will notice that they are in the reverse order of finality. In the first case everyone is aware that the coffin is irretrievably gone. In the second case it can no longer be seen, and at least symbolically has gone. In the third case it has plainly not gone. Indeed, relatives will frequently turn at the door of the chapel to see that coffin once more: it has not gone. There is no real, final, farewell. And I am told that those who choose this third pattern for ending the service sometimes find the greater difficulty later in accepting the finality of the death that has taken place.

Donating human organs for transplantation

Since the practice of transplanting human organs from one individual to another had not even been dreamed of in biblical times, there is, obviously, no direct guidance for us on the subject. So this bit of the book cannot be very well supported by texts!

We have already seen that the resurrection body is a *spiritual* body, not a *material* body, and that although the spiritual body is directly related to the material body it does not make use of any of the molecules of the old body. We should remember, as well, that all of these bodies of ours eventually crumble to dust and, given the passage of sufficient time, become scattered. Some of us have lost bits of our bodies already: my appendix has gone, and so has a good part of my stomach. Other people have been much more unfortunate and have lost eyes, hands, even legs. But we will not be in any way at a disadvantage when it comes to the resurrection, as though any parts missing from the material body will also be missing from the spiritual body.

So what have we to say about such things as donating the eye's cornea, or the kidneys, or even the heart for transplant into another human being? Well, first, we must all make up our own minds on the subject, and then decide firmly not to criticise others who may disagree with us. This is, obviously, a very personal matter. Second, we can say that we have no further use for these organs. And if they are left to the normal process they will either be uselessly cremated or equally uselessly buried. Third, we know that because of the possibility of transplanting organs, people who would otherwise be blind can see, people who would otherwise have died are alive. We can scarcely imagine the ecstatic joy of a mother who finds that a transplant that will save her son's life is possible; the enormous relief of someone slowly but inexorably going blind to recover that infinitely precious gift of sight. Surely to make such ecstasy possible is a Christian act?

But on the horizon I can see a problem. It hasn't appeared seriously yet, but it may well come: the possibility of a brain transplant. Now I must say at once: my brain isn't *me*. But it is the place, the physical location, which is most nearly me. In the brain are stored all those memories that make me 'me'. I *use* the brain, it isn't *me*. But if I die, and before the neuron patterns can dissolve that brain is transferred to another person, or if even part of my brain is transferred to another person, are we somehow creating another person who owns what are at present *my* memories, and if so just *who is that other person?*

We have now reached the point where we all need to think more deeply than we have been required to think before. Medical care in the past has been fairly straight forward. There were medicines to be taken, broken bones to be repaired, malfunctioning bits of the human body to be corrected. But now things have changed radically. We can borrow bits from other bodies, we can interfere with the normal process of conception and start a baby's existence in a test-tube. Through our knowledge of genetics we can even think of custom-designed babies. But these new processes are enormously expensive.

Just two things need to be said. First, that we will never be able to find the money to do for everyone in the world what medical science is actually capable of. I was in a mission hospital in Africa, waiting to speak to the doctor. He was talking with a lady, and when eventually they had finished their conversation, I saw that she walked away, crying. I asked the doctor about her:

'I've sent her back to her home, to die.'

'Couldn't you do anything for her?'

'Oh yes, I could. But it would take so much of my time and so much time from my nurses that we would have to neglect other cases just to care for her. I simply can't find the staff for all the needs I have.'

That dilemma used to be the dilemma of medical care in the Third World. Now it is also the dilemma of our own doctors.

The second thing to be said is that Christians need to start asking *seriously* whether some of the things that *can* be done *should* be done. And this is particularly true of experiments on embryos, on babies before they are born. There is a very useful book edited by Nigel Cameron, *Embryos and Ethics*, which is a discussion of the Warnock Report. Thinking Christians ought to read it.

The funeral service

Obviously every funeral service must be unique, just as every marriage service has to be unique. With the marriage service the couple are there and can make sure that things are done the way they had planned. With the funeral service that individual whose life we commemorate has gone. And nine times out of ten nothing has been left behind by way of instruction about the funeral. As I have said already, I have left instructions about my funeral and I hope that when the time comes the letter will be found easily and the suggestions I have made taken seriously.

The details of a funeral service can only be worked out properly when you have some idea of how many people are likely to be present and how many of them are likely to sing any hymns that have been chosen. It can be depressing to have good hymns chosen, but such a small congregation that no-one feels able to sing them. And again, I think that many hymns are pitched too high for men to sing: so it's good to try to ensure that any hymns chosen are pitched so that everyone can join in. Funerals and weddings are not the places for learning new hymns – the hymns chosen should be well known to those who will be there. A while back every wedding I went to that involved people who weren't Christians featured 'Morning has broken' because that had been the one acceptable hymn used in their school assemblies!

The most commonly sung hymn at funerals is undoubtedly 'The Lord's my shepherd'; not only is the tune fairly well known, but the third verse can be very comforting:

> Yea, though I walk in death's dark vale,
> Yet will I fear none ill;
> For Thou art with me; and Thy rod
> And staff me comfort still.

To me one of the great songs for such occasions is, 'For all the saints who from their labours rest'. Although it's a long one, it has an inspiring tune, especially with an organist who knows how to lead a congregation onwards into the last two great verses:

> But lo! there breaks a yet more glorious day;
> The saints triumphant rise in bright array;
> The King of glory passes on his way,
> Hallelujah!
>
> From earth's wide bounds, from ocean's farthest coast,
> Through gates of pearl streams in the countless host,
> Singing to Father, Son and Holy Ghost,
> Hallelujah!

> (*W Walsham How*)

There will also be a reading from the Bible. One commonly chosen is 1 Corinthians 15 but, if the speaker were able to explain the imagery, I would prefer 2 Corinthians 4:7–5:10, which has all the elements of the frailty of the present life, the nature of death itself, the promise of an eternal home, and a gentle reminder of judgment. And then of course there are those moving and triumphant words from Revelation 21:

> Then I saw a new heaven and a new earth, for the first heaven and the first earth had passed away, and there was no longer any sea. I saw the holy city, the new Jerusalem, coming down out of heaven from God, prepared as a bride beautifully dressed for her husband. And I heard a loud voice from the throne saying,

> 'Now the dwelling of God is with men, and he will live with them. They will be his people, and God himself will be with them and be their God. He will wipe every tear from their eyes. There will be no more death or mourning or crying or pain, for the old order of things has passed away.'
> *verses 1–4*

Finally, the funeral service should be neither too short, so that it lacks respect, nor too long, so that it exhausts the bereaved relatives, probably already tired through the stresses inseparable from a death. Anyone conducting a funeral in a crematorium should be aware of the fact that only a very limited time is allowed for each service, and it is very wrong to go beyond that, so causing distress to those waiting for the next funeral.

Chapter Eight

DEATH AND CHILDREN

Kids tend to think of death as a game to play...
Billy Graham

The death of small children

We have quite rightly insisted that a baby is a *person* even before being born. For myself, a baby is a *person* from conception. I am entirely opposed to experiments with what are coldly called embryos, because they are, in fact, experiments with *persons*. I accept that there may well be situations where abortion is necessary, but abortion does mean the loss of a *person*. Sadly, babies sometimes die before birth or shortly after birth, or in the early years of life. My wife and I lost our third child through a miscarriage.

This leads into profound questions of death and little children. I suppose that there are some people around who would say that a child who dies before having made a personal commitment to Christ goes to hell, but it's a long time since I met such a person. We sense that that can't be right. And so we have developed various ways of dealing with the problem. Sometimes infant baptism is seen as a way of removing any sin that might be thought to be present. Or children might be assumed to be innocent of sin until they reach some 'age of discernment', when they are deemed able to recognise the difference between right and wrong and to take responsibility for their choices. The various theories don't really have much to commend them: they recognise the problem, but the answers are not very convincing.

Perhaps the best way of handling the problem is simply to agree that God is a God of love who could not wish the eternal condemnation of a babe. But what each of these explanations is saying is that salvation depends ultimately on the mercy of God, and that we cannot conceive of God doing something that even we poor human beings can see would be unjust.

There is just a faint hint of all this in the account of the death of the baby born to David and Bathsheba (2 Samuel chapters 11–12). The chapters begin with mere sloth (it was the time when kings went to war, but David went to bed, 11:1–2). It moves on to adultery (11:4), then to hypocrisy (11:6–13), then to murder (11:14–25) and chapter 11 ends with marriage and the birth of a son. But David is king, chosen by God, leader of the people. The people knew perfectly well what was going on. He is setting a cynical example for the people to follow, but he is to be stopped. Nathan the prophet is chosen to tell him the consequences of his behaviour: the child will die. And die he does (12:18). At that point David is forced to look at the situation: 'I will go to him, but he will not return to me' (12:23). Now it could be that David is simply saying, 'He is dead. I will die'. But David *did* believe in life beyond the grave. As Herbert Lockyer put it:

> Excessive grief had been David's while the child's life was in the balance, but once dead the king knew that his grief could not bring the babe back. So, resigning himself to the will of God, David was consoled to know that heaven held a treasure for him.
>
> (*Lockyer, 1967, p 73*)

It doesn't resolve the problem of the great mystery of suffering, but there *is* a certain consolation in the belief that 'heaven has a treasure of mine'.

This profoundly moving question of how to cope with the death of a baby is beautifully dealt with in a little book by Paul Arnott, *No Time to Say Goodbye* (Lion publishing). Paul and his wife Rosanne lost their little boy, James, when he was nine weeks old. It was a cot death. No cause of his death could be determined. Sensitively, Paul puts down his own feelings and reactions, not insisting that everyone must follow the same route, but making the *pain* of it all so comfortingly clear. If denial, guilt, anger and grief, are part of any experience of death, these emotions are there a thousandfold in the death of a child. The long road back to normality begins with acceptance: he is gone from us. *I shall go to him, but he will not return to me.*

With a very late miscarriage the question about a funeral may arise. One morning I had a phone call from a friend to say that his wife had lost their baby. Could I go to the hospital to help them both in their grief? At the hospital there was the usual routine efficiency. There was no need for him to worry about the babe. The hospital would see to all that. But Roger (not his name) didn't want the hospital to see to all that. He wanted to see the little body reverently laid to rest. So we made the arrangements and Roger and I drove out to the cemetery later that day. Just the two of us. And there we said our farewells. I'm glad that we were able to do that. Of course it isn't always appropriate, but for Roger it was.

I very much like the suggestion by Paul Arnott that the deep grieving process can be helped by producing a kind of journal or biography, that tells everything that can be told about the brief life that is now over. Just writing the memories down can help to heal the hurts. To set in the handful of photographs, to include, maybe, a strand or two of hair ... years later there can be such comfort from these tender reminders. For I don't think that we ever quite forget such profound experiences.

What do we tell our children?

What do we tell our children? The first principle is that we tell them the truth, and the second is that we tell them as much as they want to know.

We must tell them the truth because some of the dodges we take refuge in actually produce more confusion – and may produce more harm – than telling them the truth. Gran has *not* gone to sleep (although it is true that the Bible itself makes use of the idea of sleep as a metaphor for death). To explain that a person who has died has 'just gone to sleep' may make sleep terrifying, and to explain that a person who has died has 'gone away for a while' makes even packing for the annual holiday frightening, because it is quite clear that what has happened is more than 'going to sleep' and more than 'going away for a while'. A trivial explanation won't do, the child will be looking for more than this and might get some sort of explanation from an unhelpful and/or unchristian, source. So we tell the truth.

Second, we tell as much as the child needs to know. We should answer the question that is being asked, and not some more complicated adult question. The answer to the question 'What happened to Jamie?' is 'Jamie has died'. And the answer to 'What is "died"?' is, 'His body stopped working'. And the answer to 'Where is Jamie?' is 'Jamie is with God, now'. But children don't usually want the whole theology of death at one go.

Children grieve. It's so easy for parents who are themselves caught up in the personal mystery of death and bereavement to forget their children and their special fears and hurts. For children it is so often the *loneliness* that is

94

the problem: Mum no longer there, and Dad so withdrawn and unhappy. They can see that something dreadful has happened, but no-one will tell them exactly *what*. Under those circumstances children will create their own explanations and interpretations of death. Sometimes they can be lurid and frightening. It is important that they should have the mystery explained, but it is also important that they should be surrounded with love and understanding, not left alone with their fears and unanswered questions.

We adults have a problem with our children, because they tend to ask the really profound questions that we dodge. They ask these questions in a logical series, trying to clear up the obscurities as they go along. 'Dad, why did Jean die?' 'Why didn't her body work properly?' 'Does your body work properly?' 'How old are you, Dad?' 'Is that really old?' 'Will I grow up to be as old as you are?' 'When will your body stop working properly?' New words must be explained, new concepts illustrated, new ideas explored. The aim is *understanding*. And the simple fact is that unless we ourselves understand we cannot explain.

In their first year at College my students often ask me why they must study such a wide range of subjects: not just Greek and Hebrew, but Philosophy, Theology, Church History and Ethics. The answer I give is always the same: 'To be able to explain simply you must understand profoundly.' We ourselves need to understand profoundly the great mystery of death, so that when our children ask we will be able to answer them simply, but correctly.

Chapter Nine

SO WHY ARE WE AFRAID?

*In World War I, British soldiers had a popular song
that went like this:*

*O death where is thy sting-a-ling-a-ling,
O grave thy victory?
The bells of hell go ting-a-ling-a-ling,
For you but not for me.*

Billy Graham

The pain of dying

It's a fact: most people are afraid of death. Or perhaps it
would be more accurate to say that most people are afraid
of dying. Sometimes this is the fear of pain associated with
some particular illness, cancer, for example. More often it
is the fear of the pain and the *indignity* of having to depend
on other people for everything, not just for meals, but
even for the most personal and intimate of needs. Older
people tend to be almost fiercely independent, often
because they have seen the consequences when others have
surrendered their independence too soon. It is generally
best to allow both the elderly and the very ill to do as
much for themselves as possible, to retain as much independence as is possible, to keep their dignity. And then,
when help is necessary it needs to be given with great

sensitivity.

Dying is the journey and death is the destination. Of course the fact is that we are already on the train. To go back to Pascal again, '*Vous êtes déjà embarqué*', 'You are already on board.' So why is there just the one stop, and why are we so scared about it? Paul gave one answer: 'The sting of death is sin' (1 Corinthians 15:56).

The sting of death

But isn't Paul wide of the mark, there? Surely the sting of death is the end of everything we have known and enjoyed down here, separation from family? Why bring sin into the picture?

First of all, for most people life isn't like that: enjoyable, fun, happy. For most people life is hard, painful, disappointing, and lonely. Huge numbers of people live their whole lives without ever having enough to eat. Millions have never known friendship. Exploitation is the common experience of most. But even so, people cling to life. They still fear death.

Of course there are those unusual circumstances where people actually welcome death. I remember driving at night time on a dirt road in Africa, when up ahead I vaguely spotted a huge dark mass spread right across the track. It was a lorry, overloaded with beer. The driver had lost control, smashed into another vehicle, and there was the whole tangled mess strewn across the road, the lorry driver thrown clear, now in agony, lying in the yellow cone of light provided by my VW Beetle's headlights. I knelt down beside the twisting body. The man was fully conscious, but in terrible pain. . .

'Go to the cab . . . look in the cab . . . you'll find my gun . . . get it, and finish me off . . . please. . .'

Well, I didn't, and the police arrived and took over the situation. And I don't know whether he lived or died. At that moment, though, he would have welcomed death in exchange for the pain. A few others I've met along the way have simply not been afraid of death.

But most people, even those for whom life is miserable, fear death. And the Bible suggests that this deep-down fear is because of 'sin'. The flat theological term 'sin' conceals instead of revealing what the problem is. Because to so many of us 'sin' means 'sex'. But that's a pathetic distortion. Sin is all those acts for which we *ought* to be sorry but defiantly *aren't* sorry for until we get near the end of the road. And often sin is what we have done to someone else. So long as we are well, and so long as *she* is well sin doesn't matter. But let death approach and suddenly it matters. Maggie Callana and Patricia Kelley record the story of 'Theresa', dying of bone cancer. She had been abandoned by her father but brought up by her mother. Her father was utterly rejected by them both. He was 'That man', until Theresa was near the end of the road. She lost control, moaned, thrashed around in her bed, but no-one could understand what she was saying. One day one word came through: 'Dad'. He was brought. He sat by her bedside and held her hand. There was nothing in the way of a conversation, but Theresa's agitation ended and a few hours later she died, peacefully (*Final Gifts*, pages 138–9). She didn't want to go with that sin still unresolved. Her sin, his sin, it didn't matter. She was involved and so she wanted to deal with it.

A second piece of the puzzle. People are afraid of death because of *sin plus judgment*. Here's our problem: we all of us expect life to be fair. We all agree that life isn't fair. And deep down inside every one of us God has put a belief in eternity; not enough to understand what eternity means, but enough for us to believe in it (Ecclesiastes 3:11). And so we work it out for ourselves: eternity is where the fairness comes in. We will all have to explain why we did what we did *to someone who knows*. That ultimate revelation of what we have really been is obviously frightening: we have never before confronted any situation where someone else knew *all* the facts and even the motives.

I remember being involved in quite a problem with a missionary. He had had a powerful disagreement with some Ethiopian Christians and the whole matter was being discussed by a Council of missionaries. 'All I ask is justice!' he announced. My only comment was: 'Look out! You may get it!' Because *I* don't want justice. What I want is grace, mercy, forgiveness, understanding, someone who will stand up for me, a good lawyer '. . . an advocate with the Father, Jesus Christ the righteous' (1 John 2:1). More than that, I want someone who can somehow foot the bill. I don't merely want a clever lawyer who can get me off on a technicality. With God as judge there won't be any 'not guilty' verdicts based on a technicality. I need the sinless Jesus who can say to the Father: 'I've settled the account.'

The alternative is justice: I get my come-uppance.

Most of us don't immediately see it like that though: more like '*He* gets *his* come-uppance'. The real baddies are dealt with: Stalin, Hitler, Saddam Hussein, murderers, people who have molested children . . . and, well, people like that. 'But *I've* never done anyone any harm . . . at least I've done my best . . . mostly. And tried to live by the Sermon on the Mount. Anyway, I'm as good as you are . . . probably better than most of those hypocrites who go to church . . . God is a God of love, isn't he? So it'll be all right, as I said, except for people like Hitler and the rest.'

Well, maybe that's how we would like it to be, but that's not the way it is. On the one side you have grace. Jesus settles the account. On the other side you have justice. And that applies to us all. You pay your own bills, in full, or else let Jesus settle the account for you. And so many people still have that lurking fear that if there *is* life after death (and they rather suspect that there is) then my past life will not look too satisfactory: not if *God* is going to examine it.

And that's what Paul meant when he wrote about *sin* being the sting of death. You have to die, you fear death, and the real problem is the lurking suspicion . . . no, let's come off the fence . . . the certainty that death isn't the end of it all. It *is* laid down that we must die 'and after that comes judgment' (Hebrews 9:27).

Romans explains

The really important part of the New Testament that deals with this theology of death (it's sometimes called 'thanatology', from a Greek word 'thanatos' meaning 'death') is Romans chapters 4–8. If you check (it depends a bit on which translation you use) you'll find that the word 'die' or 'death' appears about fifty times in these chapters. So, clearly, chapters 4–8 have a major concern with 'death'.

At the end of chapter 4 Paul says about Jesus:

> He was delivered over to death for our sins
> and was raised to life for our justification.

This sets the subject for all that is going to be said in the next four chapters. We have sinned. Christ has died because of our sins. His resurrection is the proof that God has now forgiven us: we are 'justified'.

Five theological statements about death

We can group the fifty references to death in these four chapters into five collections. The first collection, drawn from chapter five, states that death entered the world because of 'one man'. The second, another small collection, confirms that death is a universal experience. The third, large, collection spread right through the four chapters, relates death and sin. The fourth collection refers to the death of Jesus. And the fifth uses the idea of death in a metaphorical way to describe the kind of life the Christian should be living – what Paul calls 'dying to sin'.

1. *Death came through the first man*. The connection is spelled out in 5:12–18. '. . . sin entered the world through one man, and death through sin' (5:12), '. . . the many died by the trespass of one man' (5:15), '. . . by the trespass of one man, death reigned'. (These statements all refer back to Genesis chapter 3). So that's where death *as we now know it* came from: from human refusal to do what God demands, from human disobedience, from contradicting God.

This very brief section is neatly summarised by 5:18:

> . . . the result of one trespass was condemnation for all.

A new condition, condemnation, death, entered into the world. It came like a Siamese twin, united with sin. You have sin, you have death.

2. *Death is the universal fact*. Next, just in case we are tempted to think that this is all unjust and that we are condemned for someone else's fault, the same passage comments:

> . . . death came to all, because all sinned (5:12).

I am an identical twin. Clifford and I really are identical. And when we were small boys we always backed one another up. Neither of us would ever betray the other. So when we had done something wrong my mother would ask us: 'Now which of you two did it?' Our invariable response was: 'Know nothing!' The result was a simple policy in our home: when either of us was in trouble we were both in trouble. Oddly enough we didn't mind. But in fact it wasn't really fair to be punished for someone else's crimes. Well, that's not how Christian theology works: we die because of our own sins. Not because of Adam's sin. (Although if you look at that argument again you'll see that we *do* die because of that one man's sin: if someone hadn't started it we *possibly* wouldn't have fallen for it. . .)

3. *Death and sin: the Siamese twins.* Paul really hammers this home: the reality of the siamese twin connection, sin and death, death and sin. '. . . sin reigned in death' (5:21), '. . . the wages of sin is death' (6:23), '. . . sin . . . which leads to death' (6:16), '. . . sin sprang to life and I died' (7:9), '. . . sin . . . deceived me, and through the commandment put me to death' (7:11), '. . . sin . . . produced death in me' (7:13), 'The mind of sinful man is death' (8:6).

But before we go any further, notice that Paul is actually using 'death' to stand for all the consequences of sin. It's not just dying that he is thinking of, but dying and dying-to-God: dying *and* living out our lives here without God. Let me take just one of those texts quoted above:

> Don't you know that when you offer yourselves to someone
> to obey him as slaves,
> you are slaves to the one whom you obey –
> whether you are slaves to sin, which leads to death,
> or to obedience, which leads to righteousness?
>
> *Romans 6:16*

Obedience leads to righteousness.
Sin leads to death.
The alternatives are clear. By 'death' Paul means everything that is the opposite of what is meant by 'righteous-

ness'. Righteousness means a good relationship with God, sin means an end to that relationship; righteousness means a clear conscience, sin means a bad conscience. Righteousness means, peace, sin means war. Righteousness means heaven, sin means hell. Righteousness means life, sin means death:

> ... for the wages of sin is death,
> but the gift of God is eternal life
> in Christ Jesus our Lord.

Romans 6:23

4. *Jesus died for us.* Now Paul is writing about a historical fact: that Jesus died for us. He saw that as the very heart of Christianity. Take that out of the way and Christianity ceases to be Christianity. It becomes something else.

True enough, Christianity can take on all sorts of unexpected forms. That has always been the genius of our faith: it adjusts to north, south, east, west; it can provide a church with symphony concerts and it can provide a church with a jazz band, or a church where all the music is *a cappella*, unaccompanied. You can have ministers and rectors and deacons and archdeacons and bishops or you can dispense with the lot of them and just have plain Christians. You can have cathedrals and you can meet in the school hall or in someone's home. But there are some things that can't be changed. It's a bit like making a lemon meringue pie. If you happen to be out of flour maybe biscuit crumbs would do. And if there are no lemons then lemon essence would be fine. But if you play around with the recipe too much the point is reached at which it stops being lemon meringue pie. You eventually have spaghetti bolognaise. The death of Christ for the sin of the world: that is the very core of Christianity.

As Paul wrote to the church at Corinth:

> For what I received I passed on to you
> as of first importance
> that Christ died for our sins according to the
> Scriptures . . .

> *1 Corinthians 15:3*

Paul doesn't here explain *how* the death of Christ dealt with sin, he contents himself with insisting that it *does*: 'Jesus . . . was delivered over to death for our sins and was raised to life for our justification' (4:25), 'Christ died for the ungodly' (5:6), 'Christ died for us' (5:8), 'We were reconciled to God through the death of his son' (5:10). The death of Christ was in one sense a substitution: he died in my place. It was in another sense a sacrifice: he died instead of some temporary, stop-gap animal sacrifice. These two illustrations make two quite different points. First, it was the paying of a debt to ransom the slaves of sin. Second, it was the ultimate identification of God the Creator with his creation: God become man, bearing *our* sin and carrying it away. These illustrations all point back to Old Testament ideas: animal sacrifices at the Temple, deliverance from slavery in Egypt, the 'escape goat' of Leviticus 16, the Servant of Isaiah 53.

No one of these illustrations completely describes the profound significance of the cross. No one of them them *explains* how it all works. Each contributes something to our understanding of the death of Jesus.

5. *We have died to sin.* This ties in with what has already been said about preparing ourselves for death. We ought to live *now* so that we can die *then* without regret. I call it *taking care of tomorrow's memories.* Today's lifestyle is tomorrow's memory. And we should have a lifestyle *now* that will not shame us *then.*

The principle is simple: 'We died to sin' (6:2), 'our old self was crucified' (6:6), 'count yourselves dead to sin' (6:11).

The problem is that we are *not* dead. Our old nature is still very much alive. Paul does not pretend that we can actually kill off sinful ideas and dismiss temptation, once and for all. But we have to *count ourselves dead to sin*. We have to be for ever saying to ourselves: 'Look, you can't do that: you are dead to sin.' And the old sinful nature will say 'Oh no I'm not', and we have to respond 'Oh yes you are and I will make that sentence of death stick! With God's help.'

In chapter seven Paul uses an illustration. He gives the example of a woman who is married. In those days wives obeyed their husbands. So she did whatever he told her to do. If he told her that she couldn't go out to the market and couldn't go to the Temple, then she couldn't. And if some other man told her she could, well, she couldn't: her husband's word was law. But if her husband died? Then all was changed. The other man could marry her. The other man could say to her: 'Go on, go to the market, go to the Temple, if that's what you feel is right.' She was free to obey her new husband.

Before I became a Christian I wasn't free. I did what this fallen human nature of mine told me to do. Sometimes I protested. Often I wanted to do something different. But it was no use: I wasn't free. Then Jesus came along and set me free from that old nature. Actually it wasn't dead, but he told me: get rid of the old nature. Turn it out of the house and, if it won't go, call on me and my Holy Spirit, and we will deal with it for you. And if it comes back, turn it out again. 'Consider yourself to be dead'.

Five theological statements about death. It entered the world by one person. Death is the great universal fact. Sin is the Siamese twin of death. Christ died for us. We are to die to sin.

The question of hell

Finally I have to talk about heaven, hell, and judgment. Chapter ten is all about heaven but there is no corresponding chapter on hell. There are two reasons for that, first, because I have been primarily writing for Christians, to enable them to understand for themselves what death means. But second, because I am very much aware of what John Stott has referred to as the *Schadenfreude* – the glee, with which some Christians speak about hell. Almost a 'serve 'em right' attitude. With John Stott I want to repudiate that way of thinking.

Christians who high-handedly consign this person or that person to hell are in serious error. Faber has it right in his hymn:

> There's a wideness in God's mercy
> like the wideness of the sea;
> there's a kindness in his justice
> which is more than liberty.
>
> For the love of God is broader
> than the measure of man's mind,
> and the heart of the eternal
> is most wonderfully kind.

The fact is that I don't know the condition of anyone at all: only God knows our hearts, only God knows *me*. I just don't know what longing there *might* be in those who seem to leave God out altogether, and I certainly can't tell what transaction might take place beween an individual and God even in the moments immediately before death. *I don't know!* So it is not for me to make confident assertions about hell and who goes there.

But let's not go to the opposite extreme and simply dismiss hell altogether on the basis of public opinion. A

Gallup poll has shown that 66% of the population believe in heaven, but in Britain only 23% believe in hell. But those statistics make not the slightest difference to the question of the existence either of heaven or of hell. If they are there then they are there! Billy Graham put it quite bluntly: 'There is an alternative to heaven' (*Facing Death*, p 220).

In recent years some evangelical Christians have begun to take more seriously the idea that the very imagery used about hell could indicate that hell doesn't go on 'for ever and ever, day after day, throughout eternity', but that the fire of hell implies destruction, annihilation. For a careful treatment of this idea see especially David Edwards and John Stott, *Essentials*, chapter six.

I have indicated in my book, *Mission and Meaninglessness*, that I find the idea of annihilation at odds with the Bible. Of course the descriptions both of heaven and of hell make use of vivid imagery and must not be taken literally. As John Stott points out you can't really have blazing fires *and* darkness! It is also true that the pictures of the joy and beauty of heaven, and the pains of hell are intended to be kept in strong contrast. But there does seem to be one point at which both the experience of those in heaven and that of those in hell is the same: it is eternal, whatever that word means. Matthew 25:46 puts it quite clearly: '*Then they (the cursed) will go away to eternal punishment, but the righteous to eternal life.*' If eternal implies the unending experience of heaven for the blessed it seems as though it also means the unending experience of hell for the others.

But the idea of 'unending' or 'everlasting' is difficult to interpret when it refers to eternity. Presumably there is no *time* as we know it in eternity. There is no sun, no night, and no time. So people do not 'go on suffering' for unending millenia. Having said which, I still don't understand how the existence of hell in a universe ruled by God can be pleasing to him. John Stott puts it with beautiful clarity:

> ... the eternal existence of the impenitent in hell
> would be hard to reconcile with the promises of God's
> final victory over evil, or with the apparently uni-
> versalistic texts which speak of Christ drawing all
> men to himself (John 12:32) and of God uniting
> all things under Christ's headship (Ephesians 1:10),
> reconciling all things to himself through Christ
> (Colossians 1:20), and bringing every knee to bow to
> Christ and every tongue to confess his lordship
> (Philippians 2:10–11), so that in the end God will be 'all
> in all' or 'everything to everybody' (1 Corinthians 15:28).
> *(Edwards & Stott, 1992, p 319)*

I agree with John Stott, and yet, like him I have to say that
these verses of the Bible don't turn me into a universalist,
someone who believes that in the end everyone gets to
heaven. I can't believe that, because the Bible speaks so
often about hell. But these texts do make me ask some
questions about our understanding of what hell actually
is. John Stott is attracted by the idea that hell is a *destruc-
tive* fire, in which the existence of Satan, the existence of
death, and the existence of those who *will not repent*, is
brought to an end: annihilation (*Essentials*, pp 314–319).
I am not convinced by this argument.

Hell and who goes there

One thing that concerns me about people in Europe is that
so few of them ever have the opportunity of hearing about
Christianity. There are TV services and the radio's
'Thought for Today', book reviews, programmes on Israel
and archaeology, vicars appearing in soaps, funeral
services forming an almost standard part of the latest
whodunits, and other programmes on Islam and Judaism,

and there are Professors of Theology discussing the Dead Sea Scrolls with other Professors of Theology, but in all this the ordinary viewer who would maybe like to know what Christianity is all about is simply lost. Lost very simply because the ordinary viewer rarely if ever gets the opportunity to hear any *connected* or *systematic* explanation of Christianity. Worse, the ordinary viewer is positively indoctrinated with a dislike of the religion that is being offered.

The importance of all this is that it appears to me that the only reason why anyone would go to hell would be because of a refusal of the way of getting to heaven. What then have we to say about people across Europe who have not the faintest idea of what *Christianity* actually is? Millions of them may well reject the Christianity they hear about, but that is very different from rejecting a Christ of whom they have never actually heard.

I have discussed this difficult and emotive issue through ten theses which were first published in an article in *The International Review of Mission* in January 1988, and then in chapter six of *Mission and Meaninglessness*, SPCK, 1990. Two of those theses may be helpful at this point. Thesis one states:

> To any reasonable person it would appear to be unjust to condemn people to an eternal hell for failing to avail themselves of a medicine of which they have never heard.

The fifth thesis explains that

> ... those who have never heard the Christian Good News overtly preached, but who perceive God's eternal power and deity in his creation and seek after him in faith may, by the grace of God, be saved through the passion of that only Saviour of whom, through no

fault of their own, they have not heard.

(Cotterell, 1990, pp 75–78)

What I am saying is that vast numbers of people have lived and died in this world without ever *really* having the Good News about Jesus presented to them in any way that they could understand. But I simply do not believe that God condemns them to an eternal hell for their ignorance. And it's no good saying that they are actually being condemned for their sin. I have sinned just as much as they have sinned, and yet I am not condemned. I am forgiven because I have heard the Good News and received it. However, these others can only be saved by the sheer grace of God and because of the death of Christ.

Some evangelical Christians find this difficult to accept, probably because they have always been told that if you haven't actually received Christ then you are lost. And yet almost all of us allow an exception for little children. I don't know of *anyone* who believes that babies that die go to hell. And yet they haven't 'received Christ'. And I don't know of anyone who believes that people who are mentally ill, and so unable to 'receive Christ' go to hell. The grace of God is sufficient for them. Well, I believe that the same grace of God is sufficient for all those who have never heard the Good News and yet have been found by God, who has revealed his own eternal nature and deity in creation (Romans 1:20), and has actually created the world in such a way that *men would seek him and perhaps reach out for him and find him, though he is not far from each one of us* (Acts 17:27).

Chapter Ten

HEAVEN

Everywhere I go people ask, 'Are you an optimist or a pessimist?' My reply is that I'm an unswerving optimist. In the words of Robert Browning, 'The best is yet to be.'

Billy Graham

I find death absolutely unacceptable and I cannot come to terms with it. I can no more conceive of utter extinction, of never, than I can conceive of infinity. I cannot believe that all that passion, wit, eloquence and rage can be deleted by something as vulgar as the heart stopping. Where have they gone?

Elspeth Barker, The Guardian, October 19, 1992

And after death? Well, as I've already indicated it seems to me that for the Christian, death is no more than a doorway through which we pass from this life to the next, a stepping out of the tent we have lived in for comparatively few years into the home that owes nothing to human builders, a home for eternity. With Billy Graham I believe that the best is yet to be.

But what is heaven *like*?

A view from a different religion

On the question of what heaven is like the Bible is astonishingly reticent. I suppose that is because all we have just now are physical eyes and physical brains and most of us can't think about spiritual things other than in material ways. Let me clarify from another book that is trying to explain the same mystery, the Qur'an. Muhammad seems to have thought of paradise as being very much like this world, but with all the constraints and limitations and consequences removed. Better food and no need to worry about where it is to come from. Better drink and no need to worry either about getting drunk now or about a headache in the morning. Better clothes. Comfortable couches. Servants. Even what look suspiciously like paradisical prostitutes:

> Companions of the Right
> (O Companions of the Right!). . .
> those are they brought nigh the Throne,
> In the Gardens of Delight. . .
> Upon close-wrought couches
> Reclining upon them, set face to face,
> Immortal youths going round about them
> With goblets and ewers, and a cup from a spring,
> (no brows throbbing, no intoxication)
> And such fruits as they shall choose,
> And such flesh of fowl as they shall desire,
> And wide-eyed houris as the likeness of hidden
> pearls,
> A recompense for that they laboured . . .
> *Sura 56:9–24*

> Surely for the godfearing awaits
> A place of security, gardens and vineyards,
> And maidens with swelling breasts, like of age,

And a cup of overflowing. . .

Sura 78:30–34

The Bible is rather different. The focus of attention is not either man or woman, but God:

> Then the angel showed me the river of the water of life, as clear as crystal, flowing from the throne of God and of the Lamb down the middle of the great street of the city. On each side of the river stood the tree of life, bearing twelve crops of fruit, yielding its fruit every month. And the leaves of the tree are for the healing of the nations. No longer will there be any curse. The throne of God and of the Lamb will be in the city, and his servants will serve him. They will see his face, and his name will be on their foreheads. There will be no more night. They will not need the light of a lamp or the light of the sun, for the Lord God will give them light. And they will reign for ever and ever.

Revelation 22:1–5

Six characteristics of heaven

The book of Revelation is certainly very difficult to interpret, but the main thrust of it is clear enough. It is written to seven churches which were situated in what is now Turkey. The Christians there were either going through violent persecution or else were expecting persecution in the very near future. In other words it was already quite clear to them all that following Jesus was not a quiet stroll on a Sunday afternoon along the banks of the river.

John is given the job of writing a 'round robin' letter, one to be read to all the Christians in those seven churches. The churches were situated in a kind of arc, and the route of the messenger carrying the letter would follow this round. Ephesus first, then Smyrna, Pergamum, Thyatira, Sardis, Philadelphia, Sardis and lastly Laodicea. The message is: 'Hold fast! God is with you in every situation! Things are not out of control! There *is* a plan! The opposition will be defeated! Judgment at the end means justice at the end! Heaven is waiting for you!' Those are the seven elements of the letter. The point being made is quite clear: the reward up ahead makes the struggle now wonderfully worthwhile.

In times of persecution it is so easy to imagine that God has failed, God has disappeared from the scene, Christianity doesn't work. John reminds us: the darkest hour of the night is just before the dawn. Hold on!

The characteristics of heaven, as John was able to share them with us, are six:

God is at the heart of heaven. John never lost sight of that. Chapter one gives us a vision of Jesus standing in the middle of seven golden oil lamps representing the whole church on earth. In chapter four, John sees the throne and hears that overwhelming song from around it:

> Worthy is the Lamb who was slain
> to receive power and wealth and wisdom and
> strength
> and honour and glory and praise.
> To him who sits on the throne and to the Lamb
> be praise and honour and glory and power
> for ever and ever, Amen!

In chapter fourteen is the vision of Jesus with the 144,000 who had particularly committed themselves to Christ's service on earth and had been 'redeemed from the earth'. On again to chapter 22, and John has never lost sight of this one fact: God, God enthroned. He is at the heart of heaven.

The second feature of heaven is that *it marks the end*

of suffering. There are no tears, there is no sorrow, death, mourning nor pain. None of those things which have characterised life for so many people throughout history. Suffering and pain was *not* God's will. It was part of the great rebellion, the consequence of a fallen world. But in heaven we see what God always intended: his people enjoying his rule in a world from which suffering has gone.

The third feature of heaven is *the absence of evil*. Obviously that is connected with the absence of pain and suffering. Sin is excluded. The sin of the people of God has been dealt with by their Saviour. The sin of those who refused the Saviour is simply not admitted into heaven: it is as banished as are the unrepentant sinners. But most significantly, just as God is at the heart of heaven, so Satan, the deceiver, is entirely banished from heaven; the permanent nature of his exclusion marked by his being cast into a symbolically burning lake.

The fourth feature of heaven is *the light that shines throughout heaven*. There is no night, only a pure clear light, the glory of God:

> He carried me away in the Spirit to a mountain, great and high, and showed me the Holy City, Jerusalem, coming down out of heaven, from God. It shone with the glory of God, and its brilliance was like that of a very precious jewel.
>
> *Revelation 21:10–11*

The darkness is over, the night is banished, sin is ended and the pure day has come. This 'glory' appears several times in the Bible. Moses saw it when he climbed Sinai to meet God (see Exodus 24:12–17). Peter and John and James saw it when Jesus was transfigured while talking with Moses and Elijah (Luke 9:28–36). It is always the symbol of the presence of God. But in heaven the light doesn't fade away, it is never withdrawn: heaven is eternally illuminated by the glory of God.

In their remarkable book *Final Gifts*, Maggie Callanan and Patricia Kelley refer again and again to the experience of people who were very very close to death and who spoke of seeing light. Beautiful light. 'Bobby' was in terrible shape physically, and for three days before his death he was unable to speak at all. But just before he died his brother Bill reported that he spoke quite clearly: *I can see the light down the road and it's beautfiul* (page 100). Or there is 'Emma', fifty years old and in a hospice. The nurse found her one day staring into space, a dreamy look on her face. *What's happening?* the nurse asked, *There's that beautiful light* (page 104).

The fifth feature of heaven is *the reversal of the Genesis fall*. Back in chapter 12 we have our attention drawn to the last fling of 'that ancient serpent, called the devil, or Satan, who leads the whole world astray' a reminder of the fall in Genesis 3. In Genesis 2:8–10 we read of a beautiful garden watered by a life-giving river. And there is the tree of life. In Revelation 22 there is 'the river of the water of life' (22:1), and on either side of the river stands the tree of life, no longer forbidden (Genesis 3:22–24) but bearing leaves which are 'for the healing of the nations'. There is a remarkable pattern to God's plan for the world, with creation and fall at one end, and a new creation and final redemption at the other end.

The sixth feature of heaven is *celebration*. In Revelation 19:9 an angel announces: 'Blessed are those who are invited to the wedding supper of the Lamb.' And back in Matthew 22 we find Jesus saying: *The Kingdom of heaven may be compared to a king who gave a marriage feast for his son.* And then he goes on to describe a typical eastern celebration: and that is what the kingdom of heaven is like! But still there is that emphasis on God. It is emphatically a Jesus celebration, not merely a non-stop party. Here we have the people of God, the community, gathered together, rejoicing, worshipping more wonderfully, more profoundly than they ever did on earth, and this community is brought together in the happiest imaginable circumstance: a wedding! How could anyone be lonely at *this* wedding! Jesus the Christ, the Lord, at last and eternally, brought together with his Church. Of course much of the description of heaven that we get in Revelation is sheer picture language. The new City of Peace is not a gigantic cube with gates on all sides and roads of solid gold populated by unending choirs led by infinite phalanxes of harpists hosting an endless banquet. So I really don't know what heaven is like, except that it has those six characteristics. What I do know is that it is wonderful.

'Clare' suffered from acute leukemia, and at the end of the road she seemed frequently to be living in another world. Her brother, Sam, like so many others before him, wanted her to tell him what it was she could see. What was it *like?*

> Clare, what's it like? Sam said, putting a hand on her cheek,
> you've got to tell me.
> Clare snuggled against her brother's hand and smiled.
> I can't, she said. You'll have to wait your turn.
> (*Callanan & Kelley, 1992, p 109*)

I was speaking at a wonderful conference of Ethiopian Christians a few years back. The Marxists were in power. Many Christians had been imprisoned and the future looked bleak. But we *sang!* How we sang! And then we had a communion service. Ministers from all the different denominations stood together at the front to serve that unforgettable communion. I sat at the front, with them, my eyes down because they were filled again and again with tears. And I watched the feet of these people coming to communion. Poor feet, unwashed feet, bare feet, feet of evangelists who had covered a myriad miles to take the good news to their people. I seemed to see those same feet treading ever upwards to glory, onwards to heaven. And I was powerfully reminded of How's great hymn:

> From earth's wide bounds, from ocean's farthest
> coast,
> Through gates of pearl streams in the countless host,
> Singing to Father, Son and Holy Ghost,
> Hallelujah!

It will be wonderful through the gate.

REFERENCES

George Beasley-Murray, *Word Biblical Commentary Volume 36*, Word Books, Waco, 1987.

Mary Bosanquet, *The Life and Death of Dietrich Bonfhoeffer*.

S G F Brandon, *The Judgement of the Dead*.

Maggie Callanan and Patricia Kelley, *Final Gifts*, Hodder & Stoughton, 1992.

Peter Cotterell, *Mission and Meaninglessness*, SPCK., 1990.

Daniel Edwards and John Stott, *Essentials*, Hodder & Stoughton, 1992.

Billy Graham, *Facing Death and the Life After*, Word, 1987.

Billy Graham, *Storm Warning*, Word, 1992.

Johann Christoph Hampe, *To Die is Gain*, Darton, Longman and Todd, 1979.

Studdert Kennedy, *The Unutterable Beauty*, Hodder & Stoughton, 1927.

Derek Kidner, *A Time To Mourn*, IVP Leicester, 1976.

Herbert Lockyer, *The Funeral Source Book*, Pickering & Inglis, 1967.

Jenifer Pardoe, *How Many Times Can You Say Goodbye?*, SPCK Triangle, 1991.

SOME HELPFUL BOOKS

Paul Arnott, *No Time to Say Goodbye*, Albatross Books, Lion, 1992. A very honest, simple and moving book written following the cot-death of his son.

Joseph Bayly, *The Last Thing We Talk About*, Scripture Union, 1978 (out of print).

Maggie Callanan and Patricia Kelley, *Final Gifts*, Hodder & Stoughton, 1992. A delicately written book which puts together the last days of those whom the authors nursed in an American hospice.

Peter Cotterell, *Mission and Meaninglessness*, SPCK, 1990. As the title suggests this book wrestles with the problem that for most people life is a struggle, and often seems not to make sense. So what is the Christian Good News?

Stephen Davis (ed), *Death and Afterlife*, Macmillan, 1989. This is heavy going, an academic argument about the evidence for the afterlife, and ranging across religions.

David Edwards and John Stott, *Essentials*, Hodder & Stoughton, 1988. Chapter six, 'The gospel for the world' is essential reading on the theology of heaven and hell.

Billy Graham, *Facing Death and the Life After*, Word, 1987. A book written by the man who has so much experience and so much faith.

Billy Graham, *Storm Warning*, Word, 1992.

Johann Christoph Hampe, *To Die is Gain*, Darton, Longman and Todd, 1979. A restrained example of the many books written on the subject of near-death experiences.

Murray Harris, *Raised Immortal*, Marshall, Morgan and Scott, 1983. A theological study written by an evangelical scholar.

C S Lewis, *A Grief Observed*, originally published by Faber in 1961, is a moving piece of introspection, made the more moving by its transparent honesty. C S Lewis commenting on his own tragic bereavement.

Jenifer Pardoe, *How Many Times Can You Say Goodbye?* SPCK Triangle, 1991. The sub-title explains the subject: 'Living with bereavement.' The book is a gem.

Leslie Weatherhead, *Life Begins at Death*, Denholm House Press, 1973. It's long since out of print, but copies are still around.